JONATHAN CAPE
PAPERBACK
JCP 44

MOURNING BECOMES ELECTRA

A Trilogy

EUGENE O'NEILL

Mourning Becomes Electra

A TRILOGY

JONATHAN CAPE
THIRTY BEDFORD SQUARE LONDON

FIRST PUBLISHED 1932
THIS PAPERBACK EDITION FIRST PUBLISHED 1966
REPRINTED 1968, 1971

JONATHAN CAPE LTD
30 BEDFORD SQUARE, LONDON WC1

ISBN 0 224 61071 6

*Printed Offset Litho and bound in Great Britain by Cox & Wyman Ltd
London, Fakenham and Reading*

To
Carlotta
my wife

Contents

7

General Scene of the Trilogy

THE action of the trilogy, with the exception of an act of the second play, takes place in or immediately outside the Mannon residence, on the outskirts of one of the smaller New England seaport towns.

A special curtain shows the house as seen from the street. From this, in each play, one comes to the exterior of the house in the opening act and enters it in the following act.

This curtain reveals the extensive grounds—about thirty acres—which surround the house, a heavily wooded ridge in the background, orchards on the right and in the immediate rear, a large flower garden and a greenhouse on the left.

In the foreground, along the street, is a line of locust and elm trees. The property is enclosed by a white picket fence and a tall hedge. A drive curves up towards the house from two entrances with white gates. Between the house and the street is a lawn. By the right corner of the house is a grove of pine trees. Farther forward, along the drive, maples and locusts. By the left corner of the house is a big clump of lilacs and syringas.

The house is placed back on a slight rise of ground about three hundred feet from the street. It is a large building of the Greek temple style that was the vogue in the first half of the nineteenth century. A white wooden portico with six tall columns contrasts with the wall of the house proper

9

which is of grey cut stone. There are five windows on the upper floor and four on the ground floor, with the main entrance in the middle, a doorway with squared transom and sidelights flanked by intermediate columns. The window shutters are painted a dark green. Before the doorway a flight of four steps leads from the ground to the portico.

The three plays take place in either spring or summer of the years 1865–1866.

Homecoming

A Play in Four Acts
Part One of the Trilogy

Mourning Becomes Electra

Characters

BRIGADIER-GENERAL EZRA MANNON.
CHRISTINE, *his wife*.
LAVINIA, *their daughter*.
CAPTAIN ADAM BRANT, *of the clipper* " *Flying Trades*."
CAPTAIN PETER NILES, *U.S. Artillery*.
HAZEL NILES, *his sister*.
SETH BECKWITH.
AMOS AMES.
LOUISA, *his wife*.
MINNIE, *her cousin*.

Scenes

ACT ONE

Exterior of the Mannon house in New England—
April, 1865.

ACT TWO

Ezra Mannon's study in the house—no time has
elapsed.

ACT THREE

The same as Act One—exterior of the house—a
night a week later.

ACT FOUR

A bedroom in the house—later the same night.

ACT ONE

SCENE. *Exterior of the Mannon house on a late afternoon in April,* 1865. *In front is the drive
which leads up to the house from the two entrances
on the street. Behind the drive the white
Grecian temple portico with its six tall columns
extends across the stage. A big pine tree is on
the lawn at the edge of the drive before the right
corner of the house. Its trunk is a black column
in striking contrast with the white columns of the
portico. By the edge of the drive, left front, is
a dense clump of lilacs and syringas. A bench is
placed on the lawn in front of this shrubbery
which partly screens anyone sitting on it from being
seen from the front of the house.*

   *It is shortly before sunset and the soft light of
the declining sun shines directly on the front of
the house, shimmering in a luminous mist on the
white portico and the grey stone wall behind,
intensifying the whiteness of the columns, the
sombre greyness of the wall, the green of the open
shutters, the green of the lawn and shrubbery,
the black and green of the pine tree. The white
columns cast black bars of shadow on the grey
wall behind them. The windows of the lower
storey reflect the sun's rays in a resentful glare.
The temple portico is like an incongruous white
mask fixed on the house to hide its sombre grey
ugliness.*

   In the distance, from the town, a band is

*heard playing " John Brown's Body." Borne
on the light puffs of wind this music is at times
quite loud, then sinks into faintness as the wind
dies.*

*From the left rear, a man's voice is heard
singing the chanty " Shenandoah "—a song that
more than any other holds in it the brooding
rhythm of the sea. The voice soon sounds nearer.
It is thin and aged, the wraith of what must once
have been a good baritone.*

> " Oh, Shenandoah, I long to hear you
> A-way, my rolling river.
> Oh, Shenandoah, I can't get near you
> Way—ay, I'm bound away
> Across the wide Missouri."

*The singer, Seth Beckwith, finishes the last line
as he enters from around the corner of the house.
Closely following him are Amos Ames, his wife
Louisa, and her cousin Minnie.*

*Seth Beckwith, the Mannons' gardener and
man of all work, is an old man of seventy-five
with white hair and beard, tall, raw-boned and
bent-shouldered, his joints stiffened by rheuma-
tism, but still sound and hale. He has a gaunt
face that in repose gives one the strange impression
of a life-like mask. It is set in a grim expression,
but his small, sharp eyes still peer at life with a
shrewd prying avidity and his loose mouth has a
strong suggestion of ribald humour. He wears
his earth-stained working clothes.*

HOMECOMING

*Amos Ames, carpenter by trade but now taking
a holiday and dressed in his Sunday best, as are
his wife and her cousin, is a fat man in his fifties.
In character he is the townsfolk type of garrulous
gossip-monger who is at the same time devoid of
evil intent, scandal being for him merely the
subject most popular with his audience.*

*His wife, Louisa, is taller and stouter than he
and about the same age. Of a similar scandal-
bearing type, her tongue is sharpened by malice.*

*Her cousin, Minnie, is a plump little woman
of forty, of the meek, eager-listener type, with a
small round face, round stupid eyes, and a round
mouth pursed out to drink in gossip.*

*These last three are types of townsfolk rather
than individuals, a chorus representing the town
come to look and listen and spy on the rich and
exclusive Mannons.*

*Led by Seth, they come forward as far as the
lilac clump and stand staring at the house. Seth,
in a mood of aged playfulness, is trying to make
an impression on Minnie. His singing has been
for her benefit. He nudges her with his elbow,
grinning.*

SETH. How's that fur singin' fur an old feller?
I used to be noted fur my chanties. (*Seeing she is
paying no attention to him but is staring with open-
mouthed awe at the house, he turns to Ames—jubil-
antly.*) By jingo, Amos, if that news is true, there
won't be a sober man in town to-night! It's our
patriotic duty to celebrate!

AMES (*with a grin*).   We'd ought to, that's sartin !

LOUISA.   You ain't goin' to git Amos drunk to-night, surrender or no surrender !   An old reprobate, that's what you be !

SETH (*pleased*).   Old nothin' !   On'y seventy-five !   My old man lived to be ninety !   Licker can't kill the Beckwiths !   (*He and Ames laugh. Louisa smiles in spite of herself.   Minnie is oblivious, still staring at the house.*)

MINNIE.   My sakes !   What a purty house !

SETH.   Wal, I promised Amos I'd help show ye the sights when you came to visit him.   'Taint everyone can git to see the Mannon place close to. They're strict about trespassin'.

MINNIE.   My !   They must be rich !   How'd they make their money ?

SETH.   Ezra's made a pile, and before him, his father, Abe Mannon, he inherited some and made a pile more in shippin'.   Started one of the fust Western Ocean packet lines.

MINNIE.   Ezra's the General, ain't he ?

SETH (*proudly*).   Ayeh.   The best fighter in the hull of Grant's army !

MINNIE.   What kind is he ?

SETH (*boastfully expanding*).   He's able, Ezra is ! Folks think he's cold-blooded and uppish, 'cause he's never got much to say to 'em. But that's only the Mannons' way. They've been top dog around here for near on two hundred years and don't let folks fergit it.

MINNIE.   How'd he come to jine the army if he's so rich ?

SETH.   Oh, he'd been a soldier afore this war. His paw made him go to West P'int. He went to the Mexican war and come out a major. Abe died that same year and Ezra give up the army and took hold of the shippin' business here. But he didn't stop there. He learned law in addition and got made a judge. Went in fur politics and got 'lected mayor. He was mayor when this war broke out but he resigned at once and jined the army again. And now he's riz to be General. Oh, he's able enough, Ezra is !

AMES.   Ayeh.   This town's real proud of Ezra.

LOUISA.   Which is more'n you kin say fur his wife. Folks all hates her ! She ain't the Mannon kind. French and Dutch descended, she is. Furrin lookin' and queer. Her father's a doctor in New York, but he can't be much of a one 'cause she didn't bring no money when Ezra married her.

SETH (*his face growing grim—sharply*).   Never mind her. We ain't talkin' 'bout her. (*Then abruptly changing the subject.*) Wal, I've got to see Vinnie. I'm goin' round by the kitchen. You wait here. And if Ezra's wife starts to run you off fur trespassin', you tell her I got permission from Vinnie to show you round.

> (*He goes off around the corner of the house, left. The three stare about them gawkily, awed and uncomfortable. They talk in low voices.*)

LOUISA. Seth is so proud of his durned old Mannons ! I couldn't help givin' him a dig about Ezra's wife.

AMES. Wal, don't matter much. He's allus hated her.

LOUISA. Ssshh ! Someone's comin' out. Let's get back here ! (*They crowd to the rear of the bench by the lilac clump and peer through the leaves as the front door is opened and Christine Mannon comes out to the edge of the portico at the top of the steps. Louisa prods her cousin and whispers excitedly.*) That's her !

> (*Christine Mannon is a tall striking-looking woman of forty but she appears younger. She has a fine, voluptuous figure and she moves with a flowing animal grace. She wears a green satin dress, smartly cut and expensive, which brings out the peculiar colour of her thick curly hair, partly a copper brown, partly a bronze gold, each shade distinct and yet blending with the other. Her face is unusual, handsome rather than beautiful. One is struck at once by the strange impression*

it gives in repose of being not living flesh but a wonderfully life-like pale mask, in which only the deep-set eyes, of a dark violet blue, are alive. Her black eyebrows meet in a pronounced straight line above her strong nose. Her chin is heavy, her mouth large and sensual, the lower lip full, the upper a thin bow, shadowed by a line of hair. She stands and listens defensively, as if the music held some meaning that threatened her. But at once she shrugs her shoulders with disdain and comes down the steps and walks off towards the flower garden, passing behind the lilac clump without having noticed Ames and the women.)

MINNIE (*in an awed whisper*). My! She's awful handsome, ain't she?

LOUISA. Too furrin lookin' fur my taste.

MINNIE. Ayeh. There's somethin' queer-lookin' about her face.

AMES. Secret lookin'—'s if it was a mask she'd put on. That's the Mannon look. They all has it. They grow it on their wives. Seth's growed it on too, didn't you notice—from bein' with 'em all his life. They don't want folks to guess their secrets.

MINNIE (*breathlessly eager*). Secrets?

LOUISA. The Mannons got skeletons in their closets same as others ! Worse ones. (*Lowering her voice almost to a whisper—to her husband.*) Tell Minnie about old Abe Mannon's brother David marryin' that French Canuck nurse girl he'd got into trouble.

AMES. Ssshh ! Shut up, can't you ? Here's Seth comin'. (*But he whispers quickly to Minnie.*) That happened way back when I was a youngster. I'll tell you later. (*Seth has appeared from around the left corner of the house and now joins them.*)

SETH. That durned nigger cook is allus askin' me to fetch wood fur her ! You'd think I was her slave ! That's what we get fur freein' 'em ! (*Then briskly.*) Wal, come along, folks. I'll show you the peach orchard and then we'll go to my greenhouse. I couldn't find Vinnie.

> (*They are about to start when the front door of the house is opened and Lavinia comes out to the top of the steps where her mother had stood. She is twenty-three but looks considerably older. Tall like her mother, her body is thin, flat-breasted and angular, and its unattractiveness is accentuated by her plain black dress. Her movements are stiff and she carries herself with a wooden, square-shouldered, military bearing. She has a flat dry voice and a habit of snapping out her words like an officer giving orders. But in spite of these*)

22

*dissimilarities, one is immediately struck
by her facial resemblance to her mother.
She has the same peculiar shade of
copper-gold hair, the same pallor and
dark violet-blue eyes, the black eyebrows
meeting in a straight line above her nose,
the same sensual mouth, the same heavy
jaw. Above all, one is struck by the
same strange, life-like mask impression
her face gives in repose. But it is
evident Lavinia does all in her power to
emphasize the dissimilarity rather than
the resemblance to her parent. She
wears her hair pulled tightly back, as if
to conceal its natural curliness, and there
is not a touch of feminine allurement in
her severely plain get-up. Her head is
the same size as her mother's, but on her
thin body it looks too large and heavy.*

SETH (*seeing her*).   There she be now.

(*He starts for the steps—then sees she has not
noticed their presence : he stops and stands
waiting, struck by something in her manner.
She is looking off right, watching her
mother who strolls through the garden
to the greenhouse. Her eyes are bleak
and hard with an intense, bitter enmity.
Then her mother evidently disappears in
the greenhouse, for Lavinia turns her
head, still oblivious of Seth and his*

friends, and looks off left, her attention caught by the band, the music of which, borne on a freshening breeze, has suddenly become louder. It is still playing " John Brown's Body." Lavinia listens, as her mother had a moment before, but her reaction is the direct opposite to what her mother's had been. Her eyes light up with a grim satisfaction, and an expression of strange vindictive triumph comes into her face.)

LOUISA (*in a quick whisper to Minnie*). That's Lavinia !

MINNIE. She looks like her mother in face— queer-lookin'—but she ain't purty like her.

SETH. You git along to the orchard, folks. I'll jine you there. (*They walk back around the left of the house and disappear. He goes to Lavinia eagerly.*) Say, I got fine news fur you, Vinnie. The telegraph feller says Lee is a goner sure this time ! They're only waitin' now fur the news to be made official. You can count on your paw comin' home !

LAVINIA (*grimly*). I hope so. It's time.

SETH (*with a keen glance at her—slowly*). Ayeh.

LAVINIA (*turning on him sharply*). What do you mean, Seth ?

SETH (*avoiding her eyes—evasively*). Nothin'— 'cept what you mean. (*Lavinia stares at him. He*

24

avoids her eyes—then heavily casual.) Where was you gallivantin' night afore last and all yesterday?

LAVINIA (*starts*). Over at Hazel and Peter's house.

SETH. Ayeh. There's where Hannah said you'd told her you was goin'. That's funny now—'cause I seen Peter out yesterday and he asked me where you was keepin' yourself.

LAVINIA (*again starts—then slowly as if admitting a secret understanding between them*). I went to New York, Seth.

SETH. Ayeh. That's where I thought you'd gone, mebbe. (*Then with deep sympathy.*) It's durned hard on you, Vinnie. It's a durned shame.

LAVINIA (*stiffening—curtly*). I don't know what you're talking about.

SETH (*nods comprehendingly*). All right, Vinnie. Just as you say. (*He pauses—then after hesitating frowningly for a moment, blurts out.*) There's somethin' been on my mind lately I want to warn you about. It's got to do with what's worryin' you— that is, if there's anythin' in it.

LAVINIA (*stiffly*). There's nothing worrying me. (*Then sharply.*) Warn me? About what?

SETH. Mebbe it's nothin'—and then again mebbe I'm right, and if I'm right, then you'd ought t'be warned. It's to do with that Captain Brant.

LAVINIA (*starts again but keeps her tone cold and collected*). What about him?

SETH. Somethin' I calc'late no one'd notice 'specially 'ceptin' me, because—— (*Then hastily as he sees someone coming up the drive.*) Here's Peter and Hazel comin'. I'll tell you later, Vinnie. I ain't got time now anyways. Those folks are waitin' for me.

LAVINIA. I'll be sitting here. You come back afterwards. (*Then her cold disciplined mask breaking for a moment—tensely.*) Oh, why do Peter and Hazel have to come now? I don't want to see anyone! (*She starts as if to go into the house.*)

SETH. You run in. I'll git rid of 'em fur you.

LAVINIA (*recovering herself—curtly*). No. I'll see them.

> (*Seth goes back around the corner of the house, left. A moment later Hazel and Peter Niles enter along the drive from left, front. Hazel is a pretty, healthy girl of nineteen, with dark hair and eyes. Her features are small but clearly modelled. She has a strong chin and a capable, smiling mouth. One gets a sure impression of her character at a glance—frank, innocent, amiable and good—not in a negative but in a positive, self-possessed way. Her brother, Peter, is very like her in character—straightforward, guileless and good-*)

26

natured. He is a heavily-built young fellow of twenty-two, awkward in movement and hesitating in speech. His face is broad, plain, with a snubby nose, curly brown hair, fine grey eyes and a big mouth. He wears the uniform of an artillery captain in the Union Army.)

LAVINIA (*with forced cordiality*). Good afternoon. How are you ? (*She and Hazel kiss and she shakes hands with Peter.*)

HAZEL. Oh, we're all right. But how are you, Vinnie, that's the question ? Seems as if we hadn't seen you for ages ! You haven't been ill, I hope !

LAVINIA. Well—if you call a pesky cold ill.

PETER. Gosh, that's too bad ! All over now ?

LAVINIA. Yes—almost. Do sit down, won't you ?

> (*Hazel sits at left of bench, Lavinia beside her in the middle. Peter sits gingerly on the right edge so that there is an open space between him and Lavinia.*)

HAZEL. Peter can stay a while if you want him to, but I just dropped in for a second to find out if you'd had any more news from Orin.

LAVINIA. Not since the letter I showed you.

HAZEL. But that was ages ago ! And I haven't had a letter for months. I guess he must have met another girl somewhere and given me the go-by. (*She forces a smile but her tone is really hurt.*)

PETER. Orin not writing doesn't mean anything. He never was much of a hand for letters.

HAZEL. I know that, but—you don't think he's been wounded, do you, Vinnie?

LAVINIA. Of course not. Father would have let us know.

PETER. Sure he would. Don't be foolish, Hazel! (*Then after a little pause.*) Orin ought to be home before long now. You've heard the good news, of course, Vinnie?

HAZEL. Peter won't have to go back. Isn't that fine?

PETER. My wound is healed and I've got orders to leave to-morrow, but they'll be cancelled, I guess. (*Grinning.*) I won't pretend I'm the sort of hero that wants to go back, either! I've had enough!

HAZEL (*impulsively*). Oh, it will be so good to see Orin again. (*Then, embarrassed, forces a self-conscious laugh and gets up and kisses Lavinia.*) Well, I must run. I've got to meet Emily. Good-bye, Vinnie. Do take care of yourself and come to see us soon. (*With a teasing glance at her brother.*) And be kind to Peter. He's nice—when he's asleep. And he has something he's just dying to ask you!

PETER (*horribly embarrassed*). Darn you! (*Hazel laughs and goes off down the drive, left front. Peter fidgets, his eyes on the ground. Lavinia watches him.*)

28

HOMECOMING

Since Hazel's teasing statement, she has visibly with-drawn into herself and is on the defensive. Finally Peter looks up and blurts out awkardly.) Hazel feels bad about Orin not writing. Do you think he really—loves her ?

LAVINIA (*stiffening—brusquely*). I don't know anything about love ! I don't want to know anything ! (*Intensely.*) I hate love !

PETER (*crushed by this but trying bravely to joke*). Gosh, then, if that's the mood you're in, I guess I better not ask—something I'd made up my mind to ask you to-day.

LAVINIA. It's what you asked me a year ago when you were home on leave, isn't it ?

PETER. And you said wait till the war was over. Well, it's over now.

LAVINIA (*slowly*). I can't marry anyone, Peter. I've got to stay at home. Father needs me.

PETER. He's got your mother.

LAVINIA (*sharply*). He needs me more ! (*A pause. Then she turns pityingly and puts her hand on his shoulder.*) I'm sorry, Peter.

PETER (*gruffly*). Oh, that's all right.

LAVINIA. I know it's what girls always say in books, but I do love you as a brother, Peter. I wouldn't lose you as a brother for anything. We've been like that ever since we were little and started

playing together—you and Orin and Hazel and I.
So please don't let this come between us.

PETER. 'Course it won't. What do you think
I am ? (*Doggedly.*) Besides, I'm not giving up
hope but what you'll change your mind in time.
That is, unless it's because you love someone
else——

LAVINIA (*snatching her hand back*). Don't be
stupid, Peter !

PETER. But how about this mysterious clipper
captain that's been calling ?

LAVINIA (*angrily*). Do you think I care anything
about that—that—— !

PETER. Don't get mad. I only meant, folks
say he's courting you.

LAVINIA. Folks say more than their prayers !

PETER. Then you don't—care for him ?

LAVINIA (*intensely*). I hate the sight of him !

PETER. Gosh ! I'm glad to hear you say that,
Vinnie. I was afraid—I imagined girls all liked
him. He's such a darned romantic-looking cuss.
Looks more like a gambler or a poet than a ship's
captain. I got a look as he was coming out of your
gate—I guess it was the last time he was here.
Funny, too. He reminded me of someone. But
I couldn't place who it was.

HOMECOMING

LAVINIA (*startled, glances at him uneasily*). No one around here, that's sure. He comes from out West. Grandfather Hamel happened to meet him in New York and took a fancy to him, and Mother met him at Grandfather's house.

PETER. Who is he, anyway, Vinnie?

LAVINIA. I don't know much about him in spite of what you think. Oh, he did tell me the story of his life to make himself out romantic, but I didn't pay much attention. He went to sea when he was young and was in California for the Gold Rush. He's sailed all over the world—he lived on a South Sea island once, so he says.

PETER (*grumpily*). He seems to have had plenty of romantic experience, if you can believe him!

LAVINIA (*bitterly*). That's his trade—being romantic! (*Then agitatedly.*) But I don't want to talk any more about him. (*She gets up and walks towards right to conceal her agitation, keeping her back turned to Peter.*)

PETER (*with a grin*). Well, I don't either. I can think of more interesting subjects.

> (*Christine Mannon appears from left, between the clump of lilacs and the house. She is carrying a big bunch of flowers. Lavinia senses her presence and whirls around. For a moment, mother and daughter stare into each other's eyes. In their whole*)

tense attitudes is clearly revealed the bitter antagonism between them. But Christine quickly recovers herself and her air resumes its disdainful aloofness.)

CHRISTINE. Ah, here you are at last ! (*Then she sees Peter, who is visibly embarrassed by her presence.)* Why, good afternoon, Peter, I didn't see you at first.

PETER. Good afternoon, Mrs. Mannon. I was just passing and dropped in for a second. I guess I better run along now, Vinnie.

LAVINIA (*with an obvious eagerness to get him off— quickly*). All right. Good-bye, Peter.

PETER. Good-bye. Good-bye, Mrs. Mannon.

CHRISTINE. Good-bye, Peter. (*He disappears from the drive, left. Christine comes forward.*) I must say you treat your one devoted swain pretty rudely. (*Lavinia doesn't reply. Christine goes on coolly.*) I was wondering when I was going to see you. When I returned from New York last night you seemed to have gone to bed.

LAVINIA. I had gone to bed.

CHRISTINE. You usually read long after that. I tried your door—but you had locked yourself in. When you kept yourself locked in all day I was sure you were intentionally avoiding me. But Annie said you had a headache. (*While she has been speaking she has come towards Lavinia until she is now*

32

within arm's reach of her. The facial resemblance, as they stand there, is extraordinary. Christine stares at her coolly, but one senses an uneasy wariness beneath her pose.) Did you have a headache?

LAVINIA. No. I wanted to be alone—to think over things.

CHRISTINE. What things, if I may ask? (*Then, as if she were afraid of an answer to this question, she abruptly changes the subject.*) Who are those people I saw wandering about the grounds?

LAVINIA. Some friends of Seth's.

CHRISTINE. Because they know that lazy old sot, does it give them the privilege of trespassing?

LAVINIA. I gave Seth permission to show them round.

CHRISTINE. And since when have you the right without consulting me?

LAVINIA. I couldn't very well consult you when Seth asked me. You had gone to New York— (*she pauses a second—then adds slowly, staring fixedly at her mother*) to see Grandfather. Is he feeling any better? He seems to have been ill so much this past year.

CHRISTINE (*casually, avoiding her eyes*). Yes. He's much better now. He'll soon be going the rounds to his patients again, he hopes. (*As if anxious to change the subject, looking at the flowers she carries.*) I've been to the greenhouse to pick these. I felt our tomb needed a little brightening. (*She nods scornfully towards the house.*) Each time I come back after being away it appears more like a sepulchre ! The " whited " one of the Bible— pagan temple front stuck like a mask on Puritan grey ugliness ! It was just like old Abe Mannon to build such a monstrosity—as a temple for his hatred. (*Then with a little mocking laugh.*) Forgive me, Vinnie. I forgot you liked it. And you ought to. It suits your temperament. (*Lavinia stares at her but remains silent. Christine glances at her flowers again and turns towards the house.*) I must put these in water. (*She moves a few steps towards the house—then turns again—with a studied casualness.*) By the way, before I forget, I happened to run into Captain Brant on the street in New York. He said he was coming up here to-day to take over his ship and asked me if he might drop in to see you. I told him he could—and stay to supper with us. (*Without looking at Lavinia, who is staring at her with a face grown grim and hard.*) Doesn't that please you, Vinnie ? Or do you remain true to your one and only beau, Peter ?

LAVINIA. Is that why you picked the flowers— because he is coming ? (*Her mother does not answer. She goes on with a threatening undercurrent in her voice.*) You have heard the news, I suppose ? It means Father will be home soon !

CHRISTINE (*without looking at her—coolly*). We've

had so many rumours lately. This report hasn't been confirmed yet, has it? I haven't heard the fort firing a salute.

LAVINIA. You will before long!

CHRISTINE. I'm sure I hope so as much as you.

LAVINIA. You can say that!

CHRISTINE (*concealing her alarm—coldly*). What do you mean? You will kindly not take that tone with me, please! (*Cuttingly.*) If you are determined to quarrel, let us go into the house. We might be overheard out here. (*She turns and sees Seth who has just come to the corner of the house, left, and is standing there watching them.*) See. There is your old crony doing his best to listen now! (*Moving to the steps.*) I am going in to rest a while. (*She walks up the steps.*)

LAVINIA (*harshly*). I've got to have a talk with you, Mother—before long!

CHRISTINE (*turning defiantly*). Whenever you wish. To-night after the Captain leaves you, if you like. But what is it you want to talk about?

LAVINIA. You'll know soon enough!

CHRISTINE (*staring at her with a questioning dread—forcing a scornful smile*). You always make such a mystery of things, Vinnie.

> (*She goes into the house and closes the door behind her. Seth comes forward from*

> *where he had withdrawn beyond the corner of the house. Lavinia makes a motion for him to follow her, and goes and sits on the bench at left. A pause. She stares straight ahead, her face frozen, her eyes hard. He regards her understandingly.*)

LAVINIA (*abruptly*). Well? What is it about Captain Brant you want to warn me against? (*Then as if she felt she must defend her question from some suspicion that she knows is in his mind.*) I want to know all I can about him because—he seems to be calling to court me.

SETH (*managing to convey his entire disbelief of this statement in one word*). Ayeh.

LAVINIA (*sharply*). You say that as if you didn't believe me.

SETH. I believe anything you tell me to believe. I ain't been with the Mannons for sixty years without learning that. (*A pause. Then he asks slowly.*) Ain't you noticed this Brant reminds you of someone in looks?

LAVINIA (*struck by this*). Yes. I have—ever since I first saw him—but I've never been able to place who—— Who do you mean?

SETH. Your Paw, ain't it, Vinnie?

LAVINIA (*startled—agitated*). Father? No! It can't be! (*Then as if the conviction were forcing itself on her in spite of herself.*) Yes ! He does—something about his face—that must be why I've had the strange feeling I've known him before—why I've felt——— (*Then tensely as if she were about to break down.*) Oh ! I won't believe it ! You must be mistaken, Seth ! That would be too——— !

SETH. He ain't only like your Paw. He's like Orin, too—and all the Mannons I've known.

LAVINIA (*frightenedly*). But why—why should he——— ?

SETH. More speshully he calls to my mind your Grandpaw's brother, David. How much do you know about David Mannon, Vinnie ? I know his name's never been allowed to be spoke among Mannons since the day he left—but you've likely heard gossip, ain't you—even if it all happened before you was born ?

LAVINIA. I've heard that he loved the Canuck nurse girl who was taking care of Father's little sister who died, and had to marry her because she was going to have a baby ; and that Grandfather put them both out of the house and then afterwards tore it down and built this one because he wouldn't live where his brother had disgraced the family. But what has that old scandal got to do with———

SETH. Wait. Right after they was throwed out they married and went away. There was

37

talk they'd gone out West, but no one knew nothin' about 'em afterwards—'ceptin' your Grandpaw let out to me one time she'd had the baby—a boy. He was cussin' it. (*Then impressively.*) It's about her baby I've been thinkin', Vinnie.

LAVINIA (*a look of appalled comprehension growing on her face*). Oh !

SETH. How old is that Brant, Vinnie ?

LAVINIA. Thirty-six, I think.

SETH. Ayeh ! That'd make it right. And here's another funny thing—his name. Brant's sort of queer fur a name. I ain't never heard tell of it before. Sounds made up to me—like short fur somethin' else. Remember what that Canuck girl's name was, do you, Vinnie ? Marie Brantôme ! See what I'm drivin' at ?

LAVINIA (*agitated, and fighting against a growing conviction*). But—don't be stupid, Seth—his name would be Mannon and he'd be only too proud of it.

SETH. He'd have good reason not to use the name of Mannon when he came callin' here, wouldn't he ? If your Paw ever guessed—— !

LAVINIA (*breaking out violently*). No ! It can't be ! God wouldn't let it ! It would be too horrible—on top of—— ! I won't even think of it, do you hear ? Why did you have to tell me ?

HOMECOMING

SETH (*calmingly*).   There now !   Don't take on,
Vinnie.   No need gettin' riled at me.   (*He waits—
then goes on insistently.*)   All I'm drivin' at is that
it's durned funny—his looks and the name—and
you'd ought fur your Paw's sake to make sartin.

LAVINIA.   How can I make certain ?

SETH.   Catch him off guard sometime and put
it up to him strong—as if you knowed it—and
see if mebbe he don't give himself away.   (*He
starts to go—looks down the drive at left.*)   Looks
like him comin' up the drive now, Vinnie.   There's
somethin' about his walk calls back David Mannon,
too.   If I didn't know it was him I'd think it was
David's ghost comin' home.   (*He turns away
abruptly.*)   Wal, calc'late I better git back to work.

> (*He walks around the left corner of the house.
> A pause.   Then Captain Adam Brant
> enters from the drive, left, front.   He
> starts on seeing Lavinia but immediately
> puts on his most polite, winning air.
> One is struck at a glance by the peculiar
> quality his face in repose has of being a
> life-like mask rather than living flesh.
> He has a broad, low forehead, framed by
> coal-black straight hair which he wears
> noticeably long, pushed back carelessly
> from his forehead as a poet's might be.
> He has a big aquiline nose, bushy eye-
> brows, swarthy complexion, hazel eyes.*

39

*His wide mouth is sensual and moody—
a mouth that can be strong and weak by
turns. He wears a moustache, but his
heavy cleft chin is clean-shaven. In
figure he is tall, broad-shouldered and
powerful. He gives the impression of
being always on the offensive or defensive,
always fighting life. He is dressed with
an almost foppish extravagance, with
touches of studied carelessness, as if a
romantic Byronic appearance were the
ideal in mind. There is little of the
obvious sea captain about him, except
his big, strong hands and his deep voice.)*

BRANT *(bowing with an exaggerated politeness).*
Good afternoon. *(Coming and taking her hand which
she forces herself to hold out to him.)* Hope you don't
mind my walking in on you without ceremony.
Your mother told me——

LAVINIA. I know. She had to go out for a
while and she said I was to keep you company
until she returned.

BRANT *(gallantly).* Well, I'm in good luck, then.
I hope she doesn't hurry back to stand watch over
us. I haven't had a chance to be alone with you
since—that night we went walking in the moonlight, do you remember?

*(He has kept her hand and he drops his voice
to a low, lover-like tone. Lavinia can-*

40

*not repress a start, agitatedly snatching
her hand from his and turning away
from him.)*

LAVINIA (*regaining command of herself—slowly*).
What do you think of the news of Lee surrendering,
Captain ? We expect my father home very soon
now. (*At something in her tone he stares at her
suspiciously, but she is looking straight before her.*)
Why don't you sit down ?

BRANT. Thank you. (*He sits on the bench at
her right. He has become wary now, feeling something strange in her attitude but not able to make her
out—casually.*) Yes, you must be very happy at
the prospect of seeing your father again. Your
mother has told me how close you've always been
to him.

LAVINIA. Did she ? (*Then with intensity.*) I
love Father better than anyone in the world.
There is nothing I wouldn't do—to protect him
from hurt !

BRANT (*watching her carefully—keeping his casual
tone*). You care more for him than for your
mother ?

LAVINIA. Yes.

BRANT. Well, I suppose that's the usual way
of it. A daughter feels closer to her father and a
son to his mother. But I should think you ought
to be a born exception to that rule.

LAVINIA. Why ?

BRANT. You're so like your mother in some ways. Your face is the very image of hers. And look at your hair. You won't meet hair like yours and hers again in a month of Sundays. I only know of one other woman who had it. You'll think it strange when I tell you. It was my mother.

LAVINIA (*with a start*). Ah !

BRANT (*dropping his voice to a reverent, hushed tone*). Yes, she had beautiful hair like your mother's, that hung down to her knees, and big, deep, sad eyes that were blue as the Caribbean sea !

LAVINIA (*harshly*). What do looks amount to ? I'm not a bit like her ! Everybody knows I take after Father !

BRANT (*brought back with a shock, astonished at her tone*). But—you're not angry at me for saying that, are you ? (*Then filled with uneasiness and resolving he must establish himself on an intimate footing with her again—with engaging bluntness.*) You're puzzling to-day, Miss Lavinia. You'll excuse me if I come out with it bluntly. I've lived most of my life at sea and in camps and I'm used to straight speaking. What are you holding against me ? If I've done anything to offend you, I swear it wasn't meant. (*She is silent, rigidly upright, staring before her with hard eyes. He*

appraises her with a calculating look, then goes on.)
I wouldn't have bad feeling come between us for
the world. I may only be flattering myself, but I
thought you liked me. Have you forgotten that
night walking along the shore ?

LAVINIA (*in a cold, hard voice*). I haven't forgotten. Did Mother tell you you could kiss me ?

BRANT. What—what do you mean ? (*But he
at once attributes the question to her naïveté—laugh-
ingly.*) Oh ! I see ! But, come now, Lavinia,
you can't mean, can you, I should have asked her
permission ?

LAVINIA. Shouldn't you ?

BRANT (*again uneasy—trying to joke it off*). Well,
I wasn't brought up that strictly and, should or
shouldn't, at any rate, I didn't—and it wasn't the
less sweet for that ! (*Then at something in her face
he hurriedly goes off on another tack.*) I'm afraid I
gabbed too much that night. Maybe I bored you
with my talk of clipper ships and my love for
them ?

LAVINIA (*dryly*). " Tall, white clippers," you
called them. You said they were like beautiful,
pale women to you. You said you loved them
more than you'd ever loved a woman. Is that
true, Captain ?

BRANT (*with forced gallantry*). Aye. But I
meant, before I met you. (*Then thinking he has at*

43

last hit on the cause of her changed attitude towards him—with a laugh.) So that's what you're holding against me, is it? Well, I might have guessed. Women are jealous of ships. They always suspect the sea. They know they're three of a kind when it comes to a man! (*He laughs again but less certainly this time, as he regards her grim, set expression.*) Yes, I might have seen you didn't appear much taken by my sea talk that night. I suppose clippers are too old a story to the daughter of a shipbuilder. But unless I'm much mistaken, you were interested when I told you of the islands in the South Seas where I was shipwrecked my first voyage at sea.

LAVINIA (*in a dry, brittle tone*). I remember your admiration for the naked native women. You said they had found the secret of happiness because they had never heard that love can be a sin.

BRANT (*surprised—sizing her up and puzzled*). So you remember that, do you? (*Then romantically.*) Aye! And they live in as near the Garden of Paradise before sin was discovered as you'll find on this earth! Unless you've seen it, you can't picture the green beauty of their land set in the blue of the sea! The clouds like down on the mountain tops, the sun drowsing in your blood, and always the surf on the barrier reef singing a croon in your ears like a lullaby! The Blessed Isles, I'd call them! You can there forget all men's dirty dreams of greed and power!

44

HOMECOMING

LAVINIA.   And their dirty dreams—of love ?

BRANT (*startled again—staring at her uneasily*).
Why do you say that ? What do you mean,
Lavinia ?

LAVINIA.   Nothing.   I was only thinking—of
your Blessed Isles.

BRANT (*uncertainly*).   Oh !   But you said——
(*Then with a confused, stupid persistence he comes
closer to her, dropping his voice again to his love-
making tone.*)   Whenever I remember those islands
now, I will always think of you, as you walked
beside me that night with your hair blowing in the
sea wind and the moonlight in your eyes ! (*He
tries to take her hand, but at his touch she pulls away
and springs to her feet.*)

LAVINIA (*with cold fury*).   Don't you touch me !
Don't you dare—— !   You liar !   You—— !
(*Then as he starts back in confusion, she seizes this
opportunity to follow Seth's advice—staring at him
with deliberately insulting scorn.*)   But I suppose it
would be foolish to expect anything but cheap
romantic lies from the son of a low Canuck nurse
girl !

BRANT (*stunned*).   What's that ? (*Then rage at
the insult to his mother overcoming all prudence—
springs to his feet threateningly.*)   Stop, damn you !—
or I'll forget you're a woman—no Mannon can
insult her while I——

45

LAVINIA (*appalled now she knows the truth*).   So—
it is true——   You are her son !   Oh !

BRANT (*fighting to control himself—with harsh
defiance*).   And what if I am ?   I'm proud to be !
My only shame is my dirty Mannon blood !   So
that's why you couldn't stand my touching you
just now, is it ?   You're too good for the son of a
servant, eh ?   By God, you were glad enough
before—— !

LAVINIA (*fiercely*).   It's not true !   I was only
leading you on to find out things !

BRANT.   Oh, no !   It's only since you suspected
who I was !   I suppose your father has stuffed
you with his lies about my mother !   But, by God,
you'll hear the truth of it, now you know who I
am——   And you'll see if you or any Mannon
has the right to look down on her !

LAVINIA.   I don't want to hear——   (*She starts
to go towards the house.*)

BRANT (*grabbing her by the arm—tauntingly*).
You're a coward, are you, like all Mannons, when
it comes to facing the truth about themselves ?
(*She turns on him defiantly.   He drops her arm and
goes on harshly.*)   I'll bet he never told you your
grandfather, Abe Mannon, as well as his brother,
loved my mother !

LAVINIA.   It's a lie !

BRANT.   It's the truth.   It was his jealous
46

revenge made him disown my father and **cheat him** out of his share of the business they'd inherited !

LAVINIA. He didn't cheat him ! He bought him out !

BRANT. Forced him to sell for one-tenth its worth, you mean ! He knew my father and mother were starving ! But the money didn't last **my** father long ! He'd taken to drink. He was **a** coward—like all Mannons—once he felt the world looked down on him. He skulked and avoided people. He grew ashamed of my mother—and me. He sank down and down and my mother worked and supported him. I can remember when men from the corner saloon would drag him home and he'd fall in the door, a sodden carcass. One night when I was seven he came home crazy drunk and hit my mother in the face. It was the first time he'd ever struck her. It made me blind mad. I hit at him with the poker and cut his head. My mother pulled me back and gave me a hiding. Then she cried over him. She'd never stopped loving him.

LAVINIA. Why do you tell me this ? I told you once I don't want to hear——

BRANT (*grimly*). You'll see the point of it damned soon ! (*Unheeding—as if the scene were still before his eyes.*) For days after, he sat and stared at nothing. One time when we were alone **he** asked **me** to forgive him hitting her. But I hated him and I wouldn't forgive him. Then one night he went out and he didn't come back. The next morning they found him hanging in a barn !

LAVINIA (*with a shudder*). Oh !

BRANT (*savagely*). The only decent thing he ever did !

LAVINIA. You're lying ! No Mannon would ever——

BRANT. Oh, wouldn't they ? They are all fine, honourable gentlemen, you think ! Then listen a bit and you'll hear something about another of them ! (*Then going on bitterly with his story.*) My mother sewed for a living and sent me to school. She was very strict with me. She blamed me for his killing himself. But she was bound she'd make a gentleman of me—like he was !—if it took her last cent and her last strap ! (*With a grim smile.*) She didn't succeed, as you notice ! At seventeen I ran away to sea—and forgot I had a mother, except I took part of her name—Brant was short and easy on ships—and I wouldn't wear the name of Mannon. I forgot her until two years ago when I came back from the East. Oh, I'd written to her now and then and sent her money when I happened to have any. But I'd forgotten her just the same—and when I got to New York I found her dying—of sickness and starvation ! And I found out that when she'd been laid up, not able to work, not knowing where to reach me, she'd sunk her last shred of pride and written to your father asking for a loan. He never answered her. And I came too late. She died in my arms. (*With vindictive passion.*) He could have saved her—and he deliberately let her die! He's as guilty of murder as anyone he ever sent to the rope when he was a judge!

LAVINIA (*springing to her feet—furiously*). You dare say that about Father! If he were here——

BRANT. I wish to God he was! I'd tell him what I tell you now—that I swore on my mother's body I'd revenge her death on him.

LAVINIA (*with cold deadly intensity*). And I suppose you boast that now you've done so, don't you?—in the vilest, most cowardly way—like the son of a servant you are!

BRANT (*again thrown off guard—furiously*). Stop, I told you, that kind of talk!

LAVINIA. She is your only means of revenge on Father, is that it?

BRANT (*stunned—stammers in guilty confusion*). What?—She?—Who?—I don't know what you're talking about!

LAVINIA. Then you soon will know! And so will she! I've found out all I wanted to from you. I'm going in to talk to her now. You wait here until I call you!

49

BRANT (*furious at her tone*). No ! Be damned if you can order me about as if I was your servant !

LAVINIA (*icily*). If you have any consideration for her, you'll do as I say and not force me to write to my father. (*She turns her back on him and walks to the steps woodenly erect and square-shouldered.*)

BRANT (*desperately now—with a grotesque catching at his lover's manner*). I don't know what you mean, Lavinia. I swear before God it is only you I——

> (*She turns at the top of the steps at this and stares at him with such a passion of hatred that he is silenced. Her lips move as if she were going to speak, but she fights back the words, turns stiffly and goes into the house and closes the door behind her.*)

(*Curtain.*)

ACT TWO

SCENE. *In the house—Ezra Mannon's study. No time has elapsed.*

The study is a large room with a stiff, austere atmosphere. The furniture is old colonial. The walls are plain plastered surfaces tinted a dull grey with a flat white dado. At rear, right, is a door leading to the hall. On the right wall is a painting of George Washington in a gilt frame, flanked by smaller portraits of Alexander Hamilton and John Marshall. At rear, centre, is an open fireplace. At left of fireplace, a bookcase filled with law books. Above the fireplace, in a plain frame, is a large portrait of Ezra Mannon himself, painted ten years previously. One is at once struck by the startling likeness between him and Adam Brant. He is a tall man in his early forties, with a spare, wiry frame, seated stiffly in an armchair, his hands on the arms, wearing his black judge's robe. His face is handsome in a stern, aloof fashion. It is cold and emotionless and has the same strange semblance of a life-like mask that we have already seen in the faces of his wife and daughter and Brant.

On the left are two windows. Between them a desk. A large table with an armchair on either side, right and left, stands at left centre, front. At right centre is another chair. There are rugs on the floor.

Outside the sun is beginning to set and its

*glow fills the room with a golden mist. As the
action progresses this becomes brighter, then turns
to crimson, which darkens to sombreness at the end.*

*Lavinia is discovered standing by the table.
She is fighting to control herself, but her face is
torn by a look of stricken anguish. She turns
slowly to her father's portrait and for a moment
stares at it fixedly. Then she goes to it and puts
her hand over one of his hands with a loving,
protecting gesture.*

LAVINIA. Poor Father !

> (*She hears a noise in the hall and moves
> hastily away. The door from the hall is
> opened and Christine enters. She is
> inwardly uneasy, but affects a scornful
> indignation.*)

CHRISTINE. Really, this unconfirmed report must
have turned your head—otherwise I'd find it
difficult to understand your sending Annie to
disturb me when you knew I was resting.

LAVINIA. I told you I had to talk to you.

CHRISTINE (*looking around the room with aversion*).
But why in this musty room, of all places ?

LAVINIA (*indicating the portrait—quietly*). Because
it's Father's room.

CHRISTINE (*starts, looks at the portrait and quickly
drops her eyes. Lavinia goes to the door and closes it.
Christine says with forced scorn*). More mystery ?

HOMECOMING

LAVINIA. You better sit down. (*Christine sits in the chair at rear centre. Lavinia goes back to her father's chair at left of table.*)

CHRISTINE. Well—if you're quite ready, perhaps you will explain.

LAVINIA. I suppose Annie told you I'd been to visit Hazel and Peter while you were away?

CHRISTINE. Yes. I thought it peculiar. You never visit anyone overnight. Why did you suddenly take that notion?

LAVINIA. I didn't.

CHRISTINE. You didn't visit them?

LAVINIA. No.

CHRISTINE. Then where did you go?

LAVINIA (*accusingly*). To New York! (*Christine starts. Lavinia hurries on a bit incoherently.*) I've suspected something—lately—the excuse you've made for all your trips there the past year, that Grandfather was ill—— (*As Christine is about to protest indignantly.*) Oh! I know he has been —and you've stayed at his house—but I've suspected lately that wasn't the real reason—and now I can prove it isn't! Because I waited outside Grandfather's house and followed you. I saw you meet Brant!

CHRISTINE (*alarmed but concealing it—coolly*).

Well, what if you did ?   I told you myself I ran into him by accident——

LAVINIA.   You went to his room !

CHRISTINE (*shaken*).   He asked me to meet a friend of his—a lady.   It was her house we went to.

LAVINIA.   I asked the woman in the basement. He had hired the room under another name, but she recognized his description.   And yours too. She said you had come there often in the past year.

CHRISTINE (*desperately*).   It was the first time I had ever been there.   He insisted on my going. He said he had to talk to me about you.   He wanted my help to approach your father——

LAVINIA (*furiously*).   How can you lie like that ? How can you be so vile as to try to use me to hide your adultery ?

CHRISTINE (*springing up—with weak indignation*). Vinnie !

LAVINIA.   Your adultery, I said !

CHRISTINE.   No !

LAVINIA.   Stop lying, I tell you !   I went up-stairs !   I heard you telling him—" I love you, Adam "—and kissing him !   (*With a cold bitter fury.*)   You vile—— !   You're shameless and evil ! Even if you are my mother, I say it !

> (*Christine stares at her, overwhelmed by this onslaught, her poise shattered for the*

moment. She tries to keep her voice indifferent but it trembles a little.)

CHRISTINE. I—I knew you hated me, Vinnie—but not as bitterly as that ! (*Then with a return of her defiant coolness.*) Very well ! I love Adam Brant. What are you going to do ?

LAVINIA. How you say that—without any shame ! You don't give one thought to Father—who is so good—who trusts you ! Oh, how could you do this to Father ? How could you ?

CHRISTINE (*with strident intensity*). You would understand if you were the wife of a man you hated !

LAVINIA (*horrified—with a glance at the portrait*). Don't ! Don't say that—before him ! I won't listen !

CHRISTINE (*grabbing her by the arm*). You will listen ! I'm talking to you as a woman now, not as mother to daughter ! That relationship has no meaning between us ! You've called me vile and shameless ! Well, I want you to know that's what I've felt about myself for over twenty years, giving my body to a man I——

LAVINIA (*trying to break away from her, half putting her hands up to her ears*). Stop telling me such things ! Let me go ! (*She breaks away, shrinking from her mother with a look of sick repulsion. A pause. She stammers.*) You—then you've always hated Father ?

CHRISTINE (*bitterly*). No. I loved him once—
before I married him—incredible as that seems
now ! He was handsome in his lieutenant's
uniform ! He was silent and mysterious and
romantic ! But marriage soon turned his romance
into—disgust !

LAVINIA (*wincing again—stammers harshly*). So
I was born of your disgust ! I've always guessed
that, Mother—ever since I was little—when I used
to come to you—with love—but you would always
push me away ! I've felt it ever since I can
remember—your disgust ! (*Then with a flare-up
of bitter hatred.*) Oh, I hate you ! It's only right
I should hate you !

CHRISTINE (*shaken—defensively*). I tried to love
you. I told myself it wasn't human not to love my
own child, born of my body. But I never could
make myself feel you were born of any body but
his ! You were always my wedding night to me
—and my honeymoon !

LAVINIA. Stop saying that ! How can you be
so—— ! (*Then suddenly—with a strange jealous
bitterness.*) You've loved Orin ! Why didn't you
hate him too ?

CHRISTINE. Because by then I had forced myself to become resigned in order to live ! And
most of the time I was carrying him, your father was
with the army in Mexico. I had forgotten him.
And when Orin was born he seemed my child, only

mine, and I loved him for that! (*Bitterly.*) I loved him until he let you and your father nag him into the war, in spite of my begging him not to leave me alone. (*Staring at Lavinia with hatred.*) I know his leaving me was your doing principally, Vinnie!

LAVINIA (*sternly*). It was his duty as a Mannon to go! He'd have been sorry the rest of his life if he hadn't! I love him better than you! I was thinking of him!

CHRISTINE. Well, I hope you realize I never would have fallen in love with Adam if I'd had Orin with me. When he had gone there was nothing left—but hate and a desire to be revenged—and a longing for love! And it was then I met Adam. I saw he loved me——

LAVINIA (*with taunting scorn*). He doesn't love you! You're only his revenge on Father! Do you know who he really is? He's the son of that low nurse girl Grandfather put out of our house!

CHRISTINE (*concealing a start—coolly*). So you've found that out? Were you hoping it would be a crushing surprise to me? I've known it all along. He told me when he said he loved me.

LAVINIA. Oh! And I suppose knowing who he was gave you all the more satisfaction—to add that disgrace!

CHRISTINE (*cuttingly*). Will you kindly come to

the point and tell me what you intend doing ? I suppose you'll hardly let your father get in the door before you tell him !

LAVINIA (*suddenly becoming rigid and cold again—slowly*). No. Not unless you force me to. (*Then as she sees her mother's astonishment—grimly.*) I don't wonder you're surprised ! You know you deserve the worst punishment you could get. And Father would disown you publicly, no matter how much the scandal cost him !

CHRISTINE. I realize that. I know him even better than you do !

LAVINIA. And I'd like to see you punished for your wickedness ! So please understand this isn't for your sake. It's for Father's. He hasn't been well lately. I'm not going to have him hurt ! It's my first duty to protect him from you !

CHRISTINE. I know better than to expect any generosity on my account.

LAVINIA. I won't tell him, provided you give up Brant and never see him again—and promise to be a dutiful wife to Father and make up for the wrong you've done him !

CHRISTINE (*stares at her daughter—a pause—then she laughs dryly*). What a fraud you are, with your talk of your father and your duty ! Oh, I'm not denying you want to save his pride—and I know how anxious you are to keep the family from more scandal ! But all the same, that's not your real reason for sparing me !

LAVINIA (*confused—guiltily*). It is !

CHRISTINE. You wanted Adam Brant yourself !

LAVINIA. That's a lie !

CHRISTINE. And now you know you can't have him, you're determined that at least you'll take him from me !

LAVINIA. No !

CHRISTINE. But if you told your father, I'd have to go away with Adam. He'd be mine still. You can't bear that thought, even at the price of my disgrace, can you ?

LAVINIA. It's your evil mind !

CHRISTINE. I know you, Vinnie ! I've watched you ever since you were little, trying to do exactly what you're doing now ! You've tried to become the wife of your father and the mother of Orin ! You've always schemed to steal my place !

LAVINIA (*wildly*). No ! It's you who have stolen all love from me since the time I was born ! (*Then, her manner becoming threatening.*) But I don't want to listen to any more of your lies and excuses ! I want to know right now whether you're going to do what I told you or not !

CHRISTINE. Suppose I refuse ! Suppose I go off openly with Adam ! Where will you and your father and the family name be after that scandal ? And what if I were disgraced myself ? I'd have the man I love, at least !

LAVINIA (*grimly*). Not for long ! Father would use all his influence and get Brant blacklisted so he'd lose his command and never get another ! You know how much the " Flying Trades " means to him. And Father would never divorce you. You could never marry. You'd be an anchor around his neck. Don't forget you're five years older than he is ! He'll still be in his prime when you're an old woman with all your looks gone ! He'd grow to hate the sight of you !

CHRISTINE (*stung beyond bearing—makes a threatening move as if to strike her daughter's face*). You devil ! You mean little—— ! (*But Lavinia stares back coldly into her eyes and she controls herself and drops her hand.*)

LAVINIA. I wouldn't call names if I were you ! There is one you deserve !

CHRISTINE (*turning away—her voice still trembling*). I'm a fool to let you make me lose my temper— over your jealous spite ! (*A pause. Lavinia stares at her. Christine seems considering something. A sinister expression comes to her face. Then she turns back to Lavinia—coldly*). But you wanted my answer, didn't you ? Well, I agree to do as you said. I promise you I'll never see Adam again after he calls this evening. Are you satisfied ?

HOMECOMING

LAVINIA (*stares at her with cold suspicion*). You seem to take giving him up pretty easily !

CHRISTINE (*hastily*). Do you think I'll ever give you the satisfaction of seeing me grieve ? Oh, no, Vinnie ! You'll never have a chance to gloat !

LAVINIA (*still suspiciously—with a touch of scorn*). If I loved anyone—— !

CHRISTINE (*tauntingly*). If ? I think you do love him—as much as you can love ! (*With a sudden flurry of jealousy.*) You little fool ! Don't you know I made him flirt with you, so you wouldn't be suspicious ?

LAVINIA (*gives a little shudder—then fiercely*). He didn't fool me ! I saw what a liar he was ! I just led him on—to find out things ! I always hated him ! (*Christine smiles mockingly and turns away, as if to go out of the room. Lavinia's manner becomes threatening again.*) Wait ! I don't trust you ! I know you're thinking already how you can fool me and break the promise you've just made ! But you better not try it ! I'll be watching you every minute ! And I won't be the only one ! I wrote to Father and Orin as soon as I got back from New York !

CHRISTINE (*startled*). About Adam ?

LAVINIA. Only enough so they'd be suspicious and watch you too. I said a Captain Brant had been calling and folks had begun to gossip.

CHRISTINE. Ah! I see what it's going to mean—that you'll always have this to hold over me and I'll be under your thumb for the rest of my life! (*She cannot restrain her rage—threateningly.*) Take care, Vinnie! You'll be responsible if—— ! (*She checks herself abruptly.*)

LAVINIA (*suspiciously*). If what?

CHRISTINE (*quickly*). Nothing. I only meant if I went off with Adam. But of course you know I won't do that. You know there's nothing I can do now—but obey your orders!

LAVINIA (*continues to stare at her suspiciously—grimly*). You ought to see it's your duty to Father, not my orders—if you had any honour or decency! (*Then brusquely.*) Brant is waiting outside. You can tell him what you've got to do—and tell him if he ever dares come here again—— ! (*Forcing back her anger.*) And see that you get rid of him right now! I'm going upstreet to get the latest news. I won't be gone more than half-an-hour and I want him out of the house by the time I get back, do you hear? If he isn't, I'll write to Father again. I won't even wait for him to come home!

> (*She turns her back on her mother and marches out the door, square-shouldered and stiff, without a backward glance. Christine looks after her, waiting until she hears the side door of the house close after her. Then she turns and stands in tense cal-*

62

*culating thought. Her face has become
like a sinister evil mask. Finally, as if
making up her mind irrevocably, she
comes to the table, tears off a slip of paper
and writes two words on it. She tucks
this paper in the sleeve of her dress and
goes to the open window and calls.*)

CHRISTINE. Adam! (*She moves towards the door
to wait for him. Her eyes are caught by the eyes of
her husband in the portrait over the fireplace. She
stares at him with hatred and addresses him vindictively, half under her breath.*) You can thank Vinnie,
Ezra!

> (*She goes to the door and reaches it just as
> Brant appears from the hall. She takes
> his hand and draws him into the room,
> closing the door behind him. One is
> immediately struck by the resemblance
> between his face and that of the portrait
> of Ezra Mannon.*)

BRANT (*glancing uneasily at her, as they come to the
centre of the room*). She knows—— ?

CHRISTINE. Yes. She followed me to New
York. And she's found out who you are too,
Adam.

BRANT (*with a grim smile*). I know. She got
that out of me—the proof of it, at any rate. Before
I knew what was up I'd given myself away.

CHRISTINE. She must have noticed your resemblance to Orin. I was afraid that might start her thinking.

BRANT (*sees the portrait for the first time. Instantly his body shifts to a fighting tenseness. It is as if he were going to spring at the figure in the painting. He says slowly :*). That, I take it, is General Mannon ?

CHRISTINE. Judge Mannon then. Don't forget he used to be a judge. He won't forget it.

BRANT (*his eyes still fixed on the portrait—comes and sits in Mannon's chair on the left of table. Unconsciously he takes the same attitude as Mannon, sitting erect, his hands on the arms of the chair—slowly :*). Does Orin by any chance resemble his father ?

CHRISTINE (*stares at him—agitatedly*). No ! Of course not ! What put such a stupid idea in your head ?

BRANT. It would be damned queer if you fell in love with me because I recalled Ezra Mannon to you !

CHRISTINE (*going to him and putting an arm around his shoulder*). No, no, I tell you ! It was Orin you made me think of ! It was Orin !

BRANT. I remember that night we were introduced and I heard the name Mrs. Ezra Mannon ! By God, how I hated you then for being his ! I thought, by God, I'll take her from him and that'll be part of my revenge ! And out of that hatred my love came ! It's damned queer, isn't it ?

CHRISTINE (*hugging him to her*). Are you going to let him take me from you now, Adam ?

BRANT (*passionately*). You ask that !

CHRISTINE. You swear you won't—no matter what you must do ?

BRANT. By God, I swear it !

CHRISTINE (*kisses him*). Remember that oath ! (*She glances at the portrait—then turns back to Brant with a little shiver—nervously.*) What made you sit there ? It's his chair. I've so often seen him sitting there—— (*Forcing a little laugh.*) Your silly talk about resemblances—— Don't sit there. Come. Bring that chair over here. (*She moves to the chair at right centre. He brings the chair at right of table close to hers.*)

BRANT. We've got to decide what we must do. The time for skulking and lying is over—and by God I'm glad of it ! It's a coward's game I have no stomach for ! (*He has placed the chair beside hers. She is staring at the portrait.*) Why don't you sit down, Christine ?

CHRISTINE (*slowly*). I was thinking—perhaps we had better go to the sitting-room. (*Then defiantly.*) No ! I've been afraid of you long enough, Ezra ! (*She sits down.*)

c   65

BRANT. I felt there was something wrong the moment I saw her. I tried my damndest to put her off the course by giving her some soft-soap—as you'd told me to do to blind her. (*Frowning*.) That was a mistake, Christine. It made her pay too much attention to me—and opened her eyes !

CHRISTINE. Oh, I know I've made one blunder after another. It's as if love drove me on to do everything I shouldn't. I never should have brought you to this house. Seeing you in New York should have been enough for me. But I loved you too much. I wanted you every possible moment we could steal ! And I simply couldn't believe that he ever would come home. I prayed that he should be killed in the war so intensely that I finally believed it would surely happen ! (*With savage intensity*.) Oh, if only he were dead !

BRANT. That chance is over now.

CHRISTINE (*slowly—without looking at him*). Yes —in that way.

BRANT (*stares at her*). What do you mean ? (*She remains silent. He changes the subject uneasily*.) There's only one thing to do ! When he comes home I'll wait for him and not give Vinnie the satisfaction of telling him. I'll tell him myself. (*Vindictively*.) By God ! I'd give my soul to see his face when he knows you love Marie Brantôme's son ! And then I'll take you away openly and laugh at him ! And if he tries to stop me—— !

(*He stops and glances with savage hatred at the portrait.*)

CHRISTINE.   What would you do then ?

BRANT.   If ever I laid hands on him, I'd kill him !

CHRISTINE.   And then ?   You would be hanged for murder !   And where would I be ?   There would be nothing left for me but to kill myself !

BRANT.   If I could catch him alone, where no one would interfere, and let the best man come out alive—as I've often seen it done in the West !

CHRISTINE.   This isn't the West.

BRANT.   I could insult him on the street before everyone and make him fight me !   I could let him shoot first and then kill him in self-defence.

CHRISTINE (*scornfully*).   Do you imagine you could force him to fight a duel with you ?   Don't you know duelling is illegal ?   Oh, no !   He'd simply feel bound to do his duty as a former judge and have you arrested !   (*She adds calculatingly, seeing he is boiling with rage.*)   It would be a poor revenge for your mother's death to let him make you a laughing-stock !

BRANT.   But when I take you off, the laugh will be on him !   You can come on the " Flying Trades."

CHRISTINE (*calculatingly reproachful*).   I don't think you'd propose that, Adam, if you stopped

67

thinking of your revenge for a moment and thought of me ! Don't you realize he would never divorce me, out of spite ? What would I be in the world's eyes ? My life would be ruined and I would ruin yours ! You'd grow to hate me !

BRANT (*passionately*). Don't talk like that ! It's a lie and you know it !

CHRISTINE (*with bitter yearning*). If I could only believe that, Adam ! But I'll grow old so soon ! And I'm afraid of time ! (*Then abruptly changing tone.*) As for my sailing on your ship, you'll find you won't have a ship ! He'll see to it you lose this command and get you blacklisted so you'll have no chance of getting another.

BRANT (*angrily*). Aye ! He can do that if he sets about it. There are twice as many skippers as ships these days.

CHRISTINE (*calculatingly—without looking at him*). If he had only been killed, we could be married now and I would bring you my share of the Mannon estate. That would only be justice. It's yours by right. It's what his father stole from yours.

BRANT. That's true enough, damn him !

CHRISTINE. You wouldn't have to worry about commands or owners' favours then. You could buy your own ship and be your own master !

BRANT (*yearningly*). That's always been my dream—some day to own my own clipper ! And

Clark and Dawson would be willing to sell the
" Flying Trades." (*Then forgetting everything in his
enthusiasm.*) You've seen her, Christine. She's as
beautiful a ship as you're a woman. Aye, the two
of you are like sisters. If she was mine, I'd take
you on a honeymoon then ! To China—and on
the voyage back, we'd stop at the South Pacific
Islands I've told you about. By God, there's the
right place for love and a honeymoon !

CHRISTINE (*slowly*). Yes—but Ezra is alive !

BRANT (*brought back to earth—gloomily*). I know
it's only a dream.

CHRISTINE (*turning to stare at him—slowly*). You
can have your dream—and I can have mine. There
is a way. (*Then turning away again.*) You remember my telling you he had written complaining of
pains about his heart ?

BRANT. You're surely not hoping——

CHRISTINE. No. He said it was nothing
serious. But I've let it be known that he has heart
trouble. I went to see our old family doctor and
told him about Ezra's letter. I pretended to be
dreadfully worried, until I got him worried too.
He's the town's worst old gossip. I'm sure everyone knows about Ezra's weak heart by this time.

BRANT. What are you driving at, Christine ?

CHRISTINE. Something I've been thinking of
ever since I realized he might soon come home.

69

And now that Vinnie—but even if we didn't have to consider her, it'd be the only way ! I couldn't fool him long. He's a strange, hidden man. His silence always creeps into my thoughts. Even if he never spoke, I would feel what was in his mind and some night, lying beside him, it would drive me mad and I'd have to kill his silence by screaming out the truth ! (*She has been staring before her— now she suddenly turns on Brant—slowly.*) If he died suddenly now, no one would think it was any-thing but heart failure. I've been reading a book in Father's medical library. I saw it there one day a few weeks ago—it was as if some fate in me forced me to see it ! (*She reaches in the sleeve of her dress and takes out the slip of paper she had written on.*) I've written something here. I want you to get it for me. (*His fingers close on it mechanically. He stares at it with a strange stupid dread. She hurries on so as not to give him time for reflection.*) The work on the " Flying Trades " is all finished, isn't it ? You sail to Boston to-morrow, to wait for cargo ?

BRANT (*dully*). Aye.

CHRISTINE. Get this at some druggist's down by the waterfront the minute you reach there. You can make up some story about a sick dog on your ship. As soon as you get it, send it to me here. I'll be on the look out, so Vinnie will never know it came. Then you must wait on the " Flying Trades " until you hear from me or I come to you —afterwards !

BRANT (*dully*). But how can you do it—so no one will suspect?

CHRISTINE. He's taking medicine. I'll give him his medicine. Oh, I've planned it carefully.

BRANT. But—if he dies suddenly, won't Vinnie

CHRISTINE. There'll be no reason for her to suspect. She's worried already about his heart. Besides, she may hate me, but she would never think——

BRANT. Orin will be coming home, too.

CHRISTINE. Orin will believe anything I want him to. As for the people here, they'd never dream of such a thing in the Mannon house! And the sooner I do it, the less suspicion there'll be! They will think the excitement of coming home and the reaction were too much for his weak heart! Doctor Blake will think so. I'll see that's what he thinks.

BRANT (*harshly*). Poison! It's a coward's trick!

CHRISTINE (*with fierce scorn now, seeing the necessity of goading him*). Do you think you would be braver to give me up to him and let him take away your ship?

BRANT. No!

CHRISTINE. Didn't you say you wanted to kill him?

BRANT. Aye ! But I'd give him his chance !

CHRISTINE. Did he give your mother her chance ?

BRANT (*aroused*). No, damn him !

CHRISTINE. Then what makes you suddenly so scrupulous about his death ? (*With a sneer.*) It must be the Mannon in you coming out ! Are you going to prove, the first time your love is put to a real test, that you're a weak coward like your father ?

BRANT. Christine ! If it was any man said that to me——— !

CHRISTINE (*passionately*). Have you thought of this side of his homecoming—that he's coming back to my bed ? If you love me as much as you claim, I should think that would rid you of any scruples ! If it was a question of some woman taking you from me, I wouldn't have qualms about which was or wasn't the way to kill her ! (*More tauntingly.*) But perhaps your love has been only a lie you told me—to take the sneaking revenge on him of being a backstairs lover ! Perhaps———

BRANT (*stung, grabbing her by the shoulders— fiercely*). Stop it ! I'll do anything you want ! You know it ! (*Then with a change to sombre grim- ness—putting the paper in his pocket.*) And you're right. I'm a damn fool to have any feeling about how Ezra Mannon dies !

HOMECOMING

CHRISTINE (*a look of exultant satisfaction comes to her face as she sees he is definitely won over now. She throws her arms around him and kisses him passionately*). Ah! Now you're the man I love again, not a hypocritical Mannon! Promise me, no more cowardly romantic scruples! Promise me!

BRANT. I promise.

> (*The boom of a cannon sounds from the fort that guards the harbour. He and Christine start frightenedly and stand staring at each other. Another boom comes, reverberating, rattling the windows. Christine recovers herself.*)

CHRISTINE. You hear? That's the salute to his homecoming! (*She kisses him—with fierce insistence.*) Remember your mother's death! Remember your dream of your own ship! Above all, remember you'll have me!—all your own— your wife! (*Then urgently.*) And now you must go! She'll be coming back—and you're not good at hiding your thoughts. (*Urging him towards the door.*) Hurry! I don't want you to meet her! (*The cannon at the fort keep booming at regular intervals until the end of the scene. Brant goes out in the hall and a moment later the front door is heard closing after him. Christine hurries from the door to the window and watches him from behind the curtains as he goes down the drive. She is in a state of tense, exultant excitement. Then, as if an idea had suddenly come to*

73

her, she speaks to his retreating figure with a strange sinister air of elation.)   You'll never dare leave me now, Adam—for your ships or your sea or your naked Island girls—when I grow old and ugly !

> (*She turns back from the window.   Her eyes are caught by the eyes of her husband in the portrait and for a moment she stares back into them, as if fascinated.   Then she jerks her glance away and, with a little shudder she cannot repress, turns and walks quickly from the room and closes the door behind her.*)
>
> (*Curtain.*)

ACT THREE

*The same as Act One, Scene One—exterior
of the Mannon house. It is about nine o'clock
at night a week later. The light of a half-
moon falls on the house, giving it an unreal,
detached, eerie quality. The pure white temple
front seems more than ever like an incongruous
mask fixed on the sombre, stone house. All the
shutters are closed. The white columns of the
portico cast black bars of shadow on the grey wall
behind them. The trunk of the pine at right is
an ebony pillar, its branches a mass of shade.*

*Lavinia is sitting on the top of the steps to
the portico. She is dressed, as before, severely
in black. Her thin figure, seated stiffly upright,
arms against her sides, the knees close together, the
shoulders square, the head upright, is like that
of an Egyptian statue. She is staring straight
before her. The sound of Seth's thin, aged
baritone mournfully singing the chanty " Shenandoah " is heard from down the drive, off right
front. He is approaching the house and the
song draws quickly nearer :*

" *Oh, Shenandoah, I long to hear you
A-way, my rolling river.
Oh, Shenandoah, I can't get near you
Way-ay, I'm bound away
Across the wide Missouri.*

" *Oh, Shenandoah, I love your daughter
A-way, my rolling river.*"

He enters right front. He is a bit drunk but holding his liquor well. He walks up by the lilacs starting the next line " Oh, Shenandoah "— then suddenly sees Lavinia on the steps and stops abruptly, a bit sheepish.

LAVINIA (*disapprovingly*). This is the second time this week I've caught you coming home like this.

SETH (*unabashed, approaches the steps—with a grin*). I'm aimin' to do my patriotic duty, Vinnie. The first time was celebratin' Lee's surrender and this time is drownin' my sorrow for the President gittin' shot ! And the third'll be when your Paw gits home !

LAVINIA. Father might arrive to-night.

SETH. Gosh, Vinnie, I never calc'lated he could git here so soon !

LAVINIA. Evidently you didn't. He'd give you fits if he caught you drunk. Oh, I don't believe he'll come, but it's possible he might.

SETH (*is evidently trying to pull himself together. He suddenly leans over towards her and, lowering his voice, asks soberly*). Did you find out anything about that Brant ?

LAVINIA (*sharply*). Yes. There's no connection. It was just a silly idea of yours.

SETH (*stares at her—then understandingly*). Wal, if you want it left that way, I'll leave it that way.

HOMECOMING

(*A pause. He continues to stand looking at her, while she stares in front of her.*)

LAVINIA (*in a low voice*). What was that Marie Brantôme like, Seth?

SETH. Marie? She was always laughin' and singin'—frisky and full of life—with something free and wild about her like an animile. Purty she was, too! (*Then he adds:*) Hair just the colour of your Maw's and yourn she had.

LAVINIA. I know.

SETH. Oh, everyone took to Marie—couldn't help it. Even your Paw. He was only a boy then, but he was crazy about her, too, like a youngster would be. His mother was stern with him, while Marie, she made a fuss over him and petted him.

LAVINIA. Father, too!

SETH. Ayeh—but he hated her worse than anyone when it got found out she was his Uncle David's fancy woman.

LAVINIA (*in a low voice, as if to herself, staring at the house*). It's all so strange! It frightens me! (*She checks herself abruptly—turns to Seth, curtly.*) I don't believe that about Father. You've had too much whisky. Go to bed and sleep it off. (*She walks up the steps again.*)

SETH (*gazes at her with understanding*). Ayeh.

(*Then warningly, making a surreptitious signal as he sees the front door opening behind her.*) Ssstt ! (*Christine appears outlined in the light from the hall. She is dressed in a gown of green velvet that sets off her hair. The light behind her glows along the edges of the dress and in the colour of her hair. She closes the door and comes into the moonlight at the edge of the steps, standing above and a little to the right of Lavinia. The moonlight, falling full on them, accentuates strangely the resemblance between their faces and at the same time the hostile dissimilarity in body and dress. Lavinia does not turn or give any sign of knowing her mother is behind her. There is a second's uncomfortable silence. Seth moves off left.*) Wal, I'll trot along !

> (*He disappears around the corner of the house. There is a pause. Then Christine speaks in a dry mocking tone.*)

CHRISTINE. What are you moon-gazing at ? Puritan maidens shouldn't peer too inquisitively into spring ! Isn't beauty an abomination and love a vile thing ? (*She laughs with bitter mockery —then tauntingly.*) Why don't you marry Peter ? You don't want to be left an old maid, do you ?

LAVINIA (*quietly*). You needn't hope to get rid of me that way. I'm not marrying anyone. I've got my duty to Father.

CHRISTINE. Duty ! How often I've heard that word in this house ! Well, you can't say I didn't

78

do mine all these years. But there comes **an** end.

LAVINIA (*grimly*). And there comes another end —and you must do your duty again !

CHRISTINE (*starts as if to retort defiantly—then says calmly*). Yes, I realize that.

LAVINIA (*after a pause—suspiciously*). What's going on at the bottom of your mind ? I know you're plotting something !

CHRISTINE (*controlling a start*). Don't be stupid, please !

LAVINIA. Are you planning how you can see Adam again ? You better not !

CHRISTINE (*calmly*). I'm not so foolish. I said good-bye once. Do you think I want to make it harder for myself ?

LAVINIA. Has it been hard for you ? I'd never guess it—and I've been watching you.

CHRISTINE. I warned you you would have **no** chance to gloat ! (*After a pause.*) When do you expect your father home ? You want me to play my part well when he comes, don't you ?—for his sake. I'd like to be forewarned.

LAVINIA. His letter said he wouldn't wait until his brigade was disbanded but would try to get leave at once. He might arrive to-night—**or** to-morrow—or the next day I don't know.

CHRISTINE. You think he might come to-night ?
(*Then with a mocking smile.*) So he's the beau
you're waiting for in the spring moonlight !
(*Then after a pause.*) But the night train got in
long ago.

LAVINIA (*glances down the drive, left front—then
starts to her feet excitedly*). Here's someone !

> (*Christine slowly rises. There is the sound of
> footsteps. A moment later Ezra Mannon
> enters from left front. He stops short in
> the shadow for a second and stands,
> erect and stiff, as if at attention, staring
> at his house, his wife and daughter.
> He is a tall, spare, big-boned man of
> fifty, dressed in the uniform of a Brigadier-
> General. One is immediately struck by
> the mask-like look of his face in repose,
> more pronounced in him than in the
> others. He is exactly like the portrait in
> his study, which we have seen in Act
> Two, except that his face is more lined
> and lean and the hair and beard are
> grizzled. His movements are exact and
> wooden and he has a mannerism of
> standing and sitting in stiff, posed atti-
> tudes that suggest the statues of military
> heroes. When he speaks, his deep voice
> has a hollow repressed quality, as if he
> were continually withholding emotion from
> it. His air is brusque and authoritative.*)

HOMECOMING

LAVINIA (*seeing the man's figure stop in the shadow —calls excitedly*). Who's that?

MANNON (*stepping forward into the moonlight*). It's I.

LAVINIA (*with a cry of joy*). Father! (*She runs to him and throws her arms around him and kisses him.*) Oh, Father! (*She bursts into tears and hides her face against his shoulder.*)

MANNON (*embarrassed—patting her head—gruffly*). Come! I thought I'd taught you never to cry.

LAVINIA (*obediently forcing back her tears*). I'm sorry, Father—but I'm so happy!

MANNON (*awkwardly moved*). Tears are queer tokens of happiness! But I appreciate your—your feeling.

CHRISTINE (*has slowly descended the steps, her eyes fixed on him—tensely*). Is it really you, Ezra? We had just given up hope of your coming to-night.

MANNON (*going stiffly to meet her*). Train was late. The railroad is jammed up. Everybody has got leave. (*He meets her at the foot of the steps and kisses her with a chill dignity—formally.*) I am glad to see you, Christine. You are looking well. (*He steps back and stares at her—then in a voice that betrays a deep undercurrent of suppressed feeling.*) You have changed, somehow. You are prettier than ever—— But you always were pretty.

CHRISTINE (*forcing a light tone*). Compliments from one's husband ! How gallant you've become, Ezra ! (*Then solicitously.*) You must be terribly tired. Wouldn't you like to sit here on the steps for a while ? The moonlight is so beautiful.

LAVINIA (*who has been hovering about jealously, now manages to worm herself between them—sharply*). No. It's too damp out here. And Father must be hungry. (*Taking his arm.*) Come inside with me and I'll get you something to eat. You poor dear ! You must be starved.

MANNON (*really revelling in his daughter's coddling but embarrassed before his wife—pulling his arm back—brusquely*). No, thanks ! I would rather rest here for a bit. Sit down, Vinnie. (*Christine sits on the top step at centre ; he sits on the middle step at right ; Lavinia on the lowest step at left. While they are doing this he keeps on talking in his abrupt sentences, as if he were trying to cover up some hidden uneasiness.*) I've got leave for a few days. Then I must go back and disband my brigade. Peace ought to be signed soon. The President's assassination is a frightful calamity. But it can't change the course of events.

LAVINIA. Poor man ! It's dreadful he should die just at his moment of victory.

MANNON. Yes ! (*Then after a pause—sombrely.*) All victory ends in the defeat of death. That's sure. But does defeat end in the victory of death ? That's what I wonder ! (*They both stare at him, Lavinia in surprise, Christine in uneasy wonder. A pause.*)

CHRISTINE. Where is Orin ? Couldn't you get leave for him too ?

MANNON (*hesitates—then brusquely*). I've been keeping it from you. Orin was wounded.

LAVINIA. Wounded ! You don't mean—badly hurt ?

CHRISTINE (*half starting to her feet, impulsively—with more of angry bitterness than grief*). I knew it ! I knew when you forced him into your horrible war—— ! (*Then sinking back—tensely.*) You needn't trouble to break the news gradually, Ezra. Orin is dead, isn't he ?

LAVINIA. Don't say that ! It isn't true, is it, Father ?

MANNON (*curtly—a trace of jealousy in his tone*). Of course it isn't ! If your mother would permit me to finish instead of jumping at conclusions about her baby—— ! (*With a grim, proud satisfaction.*) He's no baby now. I've made a man of him. He did one of the bravest things I've seen in the war. He was wounded in the head—a close shave but it turned out only a scratch. But he got brain fever from the shock. He's all right now. He was in a rundown condition, they say at the hospital.

I never guessed it. Nerves. I wouldn't notice nerves. He's always been restless. (*Half turning to Christine.*) He gets that from you.

CHRISTINE. When will he be well enough to come home?

MANNON. Soon. The doctor advised a few more days' rest. He's still weak. He was out of his head for a long time. Acted as if he were a little boy again. Seemed to think you were with him. That is, he kept talking to " Mother."

CHRISTINE (*with a tense intake of breath*). Ah !

LAVINIA (*pityingly—with a tinge of scorn in her voice*). Poor Orin !

MANNON. I don't want you to baby him when he comes home, Christine. It would be bad for him to get tied to your apron-strings again.

CHRISTINE. You needn't worry. That passed— when he left me. (*Another pause. Then Lavinia speaks.*)

LAVINIA. How is the trouble with your heart, Father ? I've been so afraid you might be making it out less serious than it really was to keep us from worrying.

MANNON (*gruffly*). If it was serious, I'd tell you, so you'd be prepared. If you'd seen as much of death as I have in the past four years, you wouldn't be afraid of it. (*Suddenly jumping to his*

84

feet—brusquely.) Let's change the subject ! I've had my fill of death. What I want now is to forget it. (*He turns and paces up and down to the right of steps. Lavinia watches him worriedly.*) All I know is the pain is like a knife. It puts me out of commission while it lasts. The doctor gave me orders to avoid worry or any over-exertion or excitement.

CHRISTINE (*staring at him*). You don't look well. But probably that's because you're so tired. You must go to bed soon, Ezra.

MANNON (*comes to a stop in his pacing directly before her and looks into her eyes—a pause—then he says in a voice that he tries to make ordinary*). Yes, I want to—soon.

LAVINIA (*who has been watching him jealously— suddenly pulling him by the arm—with a childish volubility*). No ! Not yet ! Please, Father ! You've only just come ! We've hardly talked at all ! (*Defiantly to her mother.*) How can you tell him he looks tired ? He looks as well as I've ever seen him. (*Then to her father, with a vindictive look at Christine.*) We've so much to tell you. All about Captain Brant. (*If she had expected her mother to flinch at this, she is disappointed. Christine is prepared and remains unmoved beneath the searching, suspicious glance Mannon now directs at her.*)

MANNON. Vinnie wrote me you'd had company. I never heard of him. What business had he here?

85

CHRISTINE (*with an easy smile*).   You had better ask Vinnie ! He's her latest beau ! She even went walking in the moonlight with him !

LAVINIA (*with a gasp at being defied so brazenly*). Oh !

MANNON (*now jealous and suspicious of his daughter*). I notice you didn't mention that in your letter, young lady !

LAVINIA.   I only went walking once with him— and that was before——   (*She checks herself abruptly.*)

MANNON.   Before what ?

LAVINIA.   Before I knew he's the kind who chases after every woman he sees.

MANNON (*angrily to Christine*).   A fine guest to receive in my absence !

LAVINIA.   I believe he even thought Mother was flirting with him.   That's why I felt it my duty to write to you.   You know how folks in town gossip, Father.   I thought you ought to warn Mother she was foolish to allow him to come here.

MANNON.   Foolish !   It was downright—— !

CHRISTINE (*coldly*).   I would prefer not to discuss this until we are alone, Ezra—if you don't mind ! And I think Vinnie is extremely inconsiderate the moment you're home—to annoy you with such ridiculous nonsense !   (*She turns to Lavinia.*)   I think you've done enough mischief. Will you kindly leave us ?

LAVINIA. No.

MANNON (*sharply*). Stop your squabbling, both of you ! I hoped you had grown out of that nonsense ! I won't have it in my house !

LAVINIA (*obediently*). Yes, Father.

MANNON. It must be your bedtime, Vinnie.

LAVINIA. Yes, Father. (*She comes and kisses him—excitedly.*) Oh, I'm so happy you're here ! Don't let Mother make you believe I—— You're the only man I'll ever love ! I'm going to stay with you !

MANNON (*patting her hair—with gruff tenderness*). I hope so. I want you to remain my little girl— for a while longer, at least. (*Then suddenly catching Christine's scornful glance—pushes Lavinia away— brusquely.*) March, now !

LAVINIA. Yes, Father. (*She goes up the steps past her mother without a look. Behind her mother, in the portico, she stops and turns.*) Don't let anything worry you, Father. I'll always take care of you.

> (*She goes in. Mannon looks at his wife who stares before her. He clears his throat as if about to say something—then starts pacing self-consciously up and down at the right of steps.*)

CHRISTINE (*forcing a gentle tone*). Sit down, Ezra. You will only make yourself more tired, keeping on your feet. (*He sits awkwardly two steps below her, on her left, turned sideways to face her. She asks with disarming simplicity :*) Now please tell me just what it is you suspect me of ?

MANNON (*taken aback*). What makes you think I suspect you ?

CHRISTINE. Everything ! I've felt your distrust from the moment you came. Your eyes have been probing me, as if you were a judge again and I were the prisoner.

MANNON (*guiltily*). I——— ?

CHRISTINE. And all on account of a stupid letter Vinnie had no business to write. It seems to me a late day, when I am an old woman with grown-up children, to accuse me of flirting with a stupid ship's captain !

MANNON (*impressed and relieved—placatingly*). There's no question of accusing you of that. I only think you've been foolish to give the gossips a chance to be malicious.

CHRISTINE. Are you sure that's all you have in your heart against me ?

MANNON. Yes ! Of course ! What else ? (*Patting her hand embarrassedly.*) We'll say no more about it. (*Then he adds gruffly :*) But I'd like you to explain how this Brant happened———

88

CHRISTINE. I'm only too glad to ! I met him at Father's. Father has taken a fancy to him for some reason. So when he called here I couldn't be rude, could I ? I hinted that his visits weren't welcome, but men of his type don't understand hints. But he's only been here four times in all, I think. And as for there having been gossip, that's nonsense ! The only talk has been that he came to court Vinnie ! You can ask anyone in town.

MANNON. Damn his impudence ! It was your duty to tell him flatly he wasn't wanted !

CHRISTINE (*forcing a contrite air*). Well, I must confess I didn't mind his coming as much as I might have—for one reason. He always brought me news of Father. Father's been ill for the past year, as I wrote you. (*Then with a twitch of the lips, as if she were restraining a derisive smile.*) You can't realize what a strain I've been under—worrying about Father and Orin and—you.

MANNON (*deeply moved, turns to her and takes her hand in both of his—awkwardly*). Christine—I deeply regret—having been unjust. (*He kisses her hand impulsively—then embarrassed by this show of emotion, adds in a gruff, joking tone.*) Afraid old Johnny Reb would pick me off, were you ?

CHRISTINE (*controlling a wild impulse to burst into derisive laughter*). Do you need to ask that ? (*A pause. He stares at her, fascinated and stirred.*)

89

MANNON (*finally blurts out*). I've dreamed of coming home to you, Christine ! (*Leans towards her, his voice trembling with desire and a feeling of strangeness and awe—touching her hair with an awkward caress.*) You're beautiful ! You look more beautiful than ever—and strange to me. I don't know you. You're younger. I feel like an old man beside you. Only your hair is the same—your strange beautiful hair I always——

CHRISTINE (*with a start of repulsion, shrinking from his hand*). Don't ! (*Then as he turns away, hurt and resentful at this rebuff—hastily.*) I'm sorry, Ezra. I didn't mean—I—I'm nervous to-night.

> (*Mannon paces to the right and stands looking at the trees. Christine stares at his back with hatred. She sighs with affected weariness and leans back and closes her eyes.*)

CHRISTINE. I'm tired, Ezra.

MANNON (*blurts out*). I shouldn't have bothered you with that foolishness about Brant to-night. (*He forces a strained smile.*) But I was jealous a bit, to tell you the truth.

> (*He forces himself to turn and, seeing her eyes are shut, suddenly comes and leans over her awkwardly, as if to kiss her, then is stopped by some strangeness he feels about her still face.*)

HOMECOMING

CHRISTINE (*feeling his desire and instinctively shrinking—without opening her eyes*). Why do you look at me like that?

MANNON (*turns away guiltily*). Like what? (*Uneasily.*) How do you know? Your eyes are shut. (*Then, as if some burden of depression were on him that he had to throw off, he blurts out heavily:*) I can't get used to home yet. It's so lonely. I've got to the feel of camps with thousands of men around me at night—a sense of protection, maybe! (*Suddenly uneasy again.*) Don't keep your eyes shut like that! Don't be so still! (*Then, as she opens her eyes—with an explosive appeal.*) God, I want to talk to you, Christine! I've got to explain some things—inside me—to my wife—try to, anyway! (*He sits down beside her.*) Shut your eyes again! I can talk better. It has always been hard for me to talk—about feelings. I never could when you looked at me. Your eyes were always so—so full of silence! That is, since we've been married. Not before, when I was courting you. They used to speak then. They made me talk—because they answered.

CHRISTINE (*her eyes closed—tensely*). Don't talk, Ezra.

MANNON (*as if he had determined, once started, to go on doggedly without heeding any interruption*). It was seeing death all the time in this war got me to thinking these things. Death was so common,

91

it didn't mean anything. That freed me to think of life. Queer, isn't it? Death made me think of life. Before that life had only made me think of death !

CHRISTINE (*without opening her eyes*). Why are you talking of death ?

MANNON. That's always been the Mannons' way of thinking. They went to the white meeting-house on Sabbaths and meditated on death. Life was a dying. Being born was starting to die. Death was being born. (*Shaking his head with a dogged bewilderment.*) How in hell people ever got such notions ! That white meeting-house. It stuck in my mind—clean-scrubbed and white-washed—a temple of death ! But in this war I've seen too many white walls splattered with blood that counted no more than dirty water. I've seen dead men scattered about, no more important than rubbish to be got rid of. That made the white meeting-house seem meaningless—making so much solemn fuss over death !

CHRISTINE (*opens her eyes and stares at him with a strange terror*). What has this talk of death to do with me ?

MANNON (*avoiding her glance—insistently*). Shut your eyes again. Listen and you'll know. (*She shuts her eyes. He plods on with a note of desperation in his voice.*) I thought about my life—lying awake nights—and about your life. In the middle of battle I'd think maybe in a minute I'll be dead. But my life as just me ending, that didn't appear worth a thought one way or another. But listen, me as your husband being killed, that seemed queer and wrong—like something dying that had never lived. Then all the years we've been man and wife would rise up in my mind and I would try to look at them. But nothing was clear except that there'd always been some barrier between us— a wall hiding us from each other! I would try to make up my mind exactly what that wall was but I never could discover. (*With a clumsy appealing gesture.*) Do you know?

CHRISTINE (*tensely*). I don't know what you're talking about.

MANNON. But you've known it was there! Don't lie, Christine! (*He looks at her still face and closed eyes, imploring her to reassure him—then blunders on doggedly.*) Maybe you've always known you didn't love me. I call to mind the Mexican War. I could see you wanted me to go. I had a feeling you'd grown to hate me. Did you? (*She doesn't answer.*) That was why I went. I was hoping I might get killed. Maybe you were hoping that too. Were you?

CHRISTINE (*stammers*). No, no, I—— What makes you say such things?

MANNON. When I came back you had turned to your new baby, Orin. I was hardly alive for you

any more. I saw that. I tried not to hate Orin.
I turned to Vinnie, but a daughter's not a wife.
Then I made up my mind I'd do my work in the
world and leave you alone in your life and not care.
That's why the shipping wasn't enough—why I
became a judge and a mayor and such vain truck,
and why folks in town look on me as so able !
Ha ! Able for what ? Not for what I wanted
most in life ! Not for your love ! No ! Able
only to keep my mind from thinking of what I'd
lost ! (*He stares at her—then asks pleadingly :*)
For you did love me before we were married. You
won't deny that, will you ?

CHRISTINE (*desperately*). I don't deny anything !

MANNON (*drawing himself up with a stern pride
and dignity and surrendering himself like a commander
against hopeless odds*). All right, then. I came
home to surrender to you—what's inside me. I
love you. I loved you then, and all the years
between, and I love you now.

CHRISTINE (*distractedly*). Ezra ! Please !

MANNON. I want that said ! Maybe you have
forgotten it. I wouldn't blame you. I guess I
haven't said it or showed it much—ever. Something queer in me keeps me mum about the things
I'd like most to say—keeps me hiding the things
I'd like to show. Something keeps me sitting
numb in my own heart—like a statue of a dead
man in a town square. (*Suddenly he reaches over*

and takes her hand.)   I want to find what that wall is
that marriage put between us !   You've got to help
me smash it down !   We have twenty good years
still before us !   I've been thinking of what we
could do to get back to each other.   I've a notion
if we'd leave the children and go off on a voyage
together—to the other side of the world—find
some island where we could be alone a while.
You'll find I have changed, Christine.   I'm sick
of death !   I want life !   Maybe you could love
me now !   (*In a note of final desperate pleading.*)
I've got to make you love me !

CHRISTINE (*pulls her hand away from him and
springs to her feet wildly*).   For God's sake, stop
talking.   I don't know what you're saying.   Leave
me alone !   What must be, must be !   You make
me weak !   (*Then abruptly.*)   It's getting late.

MANNON (*terribly wounded, withdrawn into his stiff
soldier armour—takes out his watch mechanically*).
Yes—six past eleven.   Time to turn in.   (*He
ascends two steps, his face towards the door.   He says
bitterly :*)   You tell me to stop talking !   By God,
that's funny !

CHRISTINE (*collected now and calculating—takes
hold of his arm, seductively*).   I meant—what is the
good of words ?   There is no wall between us.   I
love you.

MANNON (*grabs her by the shoulders and stares into
her face*).   Christine !   I'd give my soul to believe
95

that—but—I'm afraid ! (*She kisses him. He presses her fiercely in his arms—passionately.*) Christine ! (*The door behind him is opened and Lavinia appears at the edge of the portico behind and above him. She wears slippers over her bare feet and has a dark dressing-gown over her night-dress. She shrinks from their embrace with aversion. They separate, startled.*)

MANNON (*embarrassed—irritably*). Thought you'd gone to bed, young lady !

LAVINIA (*woodenly*). I didn't feel sleepy. I thought I'd walk a little. It's such a fine night.

CHRISTINE. We are just going to bed. Your father is tired. (*She moves up, past her daughter, taking Mannon's hand, leading him after her to the door.*)

MANNON. No time for a walk, if you ask me. See you turn in soon.

LAVINIA. Yes, Father.

MANNON. Good night.

> (*The door closes behind them. Lavinia stands staring before her—then walks stiffly down the steps and stands again. Light appears between the chinks of the shutters in the bedroom on the second floor to the left. She looks up.*)

LAVINIA (*in an anguish of jealous hatred*). I hate you ! You steal even Father's love from me again !

You stole all love from me when I was born ! (*Then almost with a sob, hiding her face in her hands.*) Oh, Mother ! Why have you done this to me ? What harm had I done you ? (*Then looking up at the window again—with passionate disgust.*) Father, how can you love that shameless harlot ? (*Then frenziedly.*) I can't bear it ! I won't ! It's my duty to tell him about her ! I will ! (*She calls desperately :*) Father ! Father ! (*The shutter of the bedroom is pushed open and Mannon leans out.*)

MANNON (*sharply*). What is it ? Don't shout like that !

LAVINIA (*stammers lamely*). I—I remembered I forgot to say good night, Father.

MANNON (*exasperated*). Good heavens ! What —— (*Then gently.*) Oh—all right—good night, Vinnie. Get to bed soon, like a good girl.

LAVINIA. Yes, Father. Good night.

> (*He goes back in the bedroom and pulls the shutter closed. She stands staring, fascinated, up at the window, wringing her hands in a piteous desperation.*)

> (*Curtain.*)

ACT FOUR

SCENE. *Ezra Mannon's bedroom. A big four-poster bed is at rear, centre, the foot front, the head against the rear wall. A small stand, with a candle on it, is by the head of the bed on the left. To the left of the stand is a door leading into Christine's room. The door is open. In the left wall are two windows. At left front is a table with a lamp on it and a chair beside it. In the right wall, front, is a door leading to the hall. Farther back, against the wall, is a bureau.*

None of these details can be discerned at first because the room is in darkness, except for what moonlight filters feebly through the shutters. It is about dawn of the following morning.

Christine's form can be made out, a pale ghost in the darkness, as she slips slowly and stealthily from the bed. She tiptoes to the table, left front, and picks up a light-coloured dressing-gown that is flung over the chair and puts it on. She stands listening for some sound from the bed. A pause. Then Mannon's voice comes suddenly from the bed, dull and lifeless.

MANNON. Christine.

CHRISTINE (*starts violently—in a strained voice*). Yes.

MANNON. Must be near daybreak, isn't it?

CHRISTINE. Yes. It is beginning to get grey.

MANNON. What made you jump when I spoke ? Is my voice so strange to you ?

CHRISTINE. I thought you were asleep.

MANNON. I haven't been able to sleep. I've been lying here thinking. What makes you so uneasy ?

CHRISTINE. I haven't been able to sleep either.

MANNON. You crept out of bed so quietly.

CHRISTINE. I didn't want to wake you.

MANNON (*bitterly*). Couldn't you bear it—lying close to me ?

CHRISTINE. I didn't want to disturb you by tossing.

MANNON. We'd better light the light and talk a while.

CHRISTINE (*with dread*). I don't want to talk ! I prefer the dark.

MANNON. I want to see you. (*He takes matches from the stand by the bed and lights the candle on it. Christine hastily sits down in the chair by the table, pushing it so she sits facing left front, with her face turned three-quarters away from him. He pushes his back up against the head of the bed in a half-sitting position. His face, with the flickering candle-light on its side, has a grim, bitter expression*). You like the

99

dark where you can't see your old man of a husband, is that it?

CHRISTINE. I wish you wouldn't talk like that, Ezra. If you are going to say stupid things, I'll go in my own room. (*She gets to her feet but keeps her face turned away from him.*)

MANNON. Wait! (*Then a note of pleading in his voice.*) Don't go. I don't want to be alone. (*She sits again in the same position as before. He goes on humbly.*) I didn't mean to say those things. I guess there's bitterness inside me—my own cussedness, maybe—and sometimes it gets out before I can stop it.

CHRISTINE. You have always been bitter.

MANNON. Before we married?

CHRISTINE. I don't remember.

MANNON. You don't want to remember you ever loved me!

CHRISTINE (*tensely*). I don't want to talk of the past! (*Abruptly changing the subject.*) Did you hear Vinnie the first part of the night? She was pacing up and down before the house like a sentry guarding you. She didn't go to bed until two. I heard the clock strike.

MANNON. There is one who loves me, at least! (*Then after a pause.*) I feel strange, Christine.

CHRISTINE. You mean—your heart ? You don't think you are going to be—taken ill, do you ?

MANNON (*harshly*). No ! (*A pause—then accusingly.*) Is that what you're waiting for ? Is that why you were so willing to give yourself to-night ? Were you hoping—— ?

CHRISTINE (*springing up*). Ezra ! Stop talking like that ! I can't stand it ! (*She moves as if to go into her own room.*)

MANNON. Wait ! I'm sorry I said that. (*Then, as she sits down again, he goes on gloomily.*) It isn't my heart. It's something uneasy troubling my mind—as if something in me was listening, watching, waiting for something to happen.

CHRISTINE. Waiting for what to happen ?

MANNON. I don't know. (*A pause—then he goes on sombrely.*) This house is not my house. This is not my room nor my bed. They are empty—waiting for someone to move in ! And you are not my wife ! You are waiting for something !

CHRISTINE (*beginning to snap under the strain—jumps to her feet again*). What would I be waiting for ?

MANNON. For death—to set you free !

CHRISTINE. Leave me alone ! Stop nagging at me with your crazy suspicions ! (*Then anger and*

hatred come into her voice.)   Not your wife !   You
acted as if I were your wife—your property—not
so long ago !

MANNON (*with bitter scorn*).   Your body ?   What
are bodies to me ?   I've seen too many rotting in
the sun to make grass greener !   Ashes to ashes,
dirt to dirt !   Is that your notion of love ?   Do
you think I married a body ?   (*Then, as if all the
bitterness and hurt in him had suddenly burst its dam.*)
You were lying to me to-night as you've always
lied !   You were only pretending love !   You let
me take you as if you were a nigger slave I'd bought
at auction !   You made me appear a lustful beast
in my own eyes !—as you've always done since
our first marriage night !   I would feel cleaner
now if I had gone to a brothel !   I would feel more
honour between myself and life !

CHRISTINE (*in a stifled voice*).   Look out, Ezra !
I won't stand——

MANNON (*with a harsh laugh*).   And I had hoped
my homecoming would mark a new beginning—
new love between us !   I told you my secret
feelings.   I tore my insides out for you—thinking
you'd understand !   By God, I'm an old fool !

CHRISTINE (*her voice grown strident*).   Did you
think you could make me weak—make me forget
all the years ?   Oh no, Ezra !   It's too late !
(*Then her voice changes, as if she had suddenly
resolved on a course of action, and becomes deliberately*

taunting.) You want the truth ? You've guessed it ! You've used me, you've given me children, but I've never once been yours ! I never could be ! And whose fault is it ? I loved you when I married you ! I wanted to give myself ! But you made me so I couldn't give ! You filled me with disgust !

MANNON (*furiously*). You say that to me ! (*Then trying to calm himself—stammers.*) No ! Be quiet ! We mustn't fight ! I mustn't lose my temper ! It will bring on—— !

CHRISTINE (*goading him with calculating cruelty*). Oh, no ! You needn't adopt that pitiful tone ! You wanted the truth and you're going to hear it now !

MANNON (*frightened—almost pleading*). Be quiet, Christine !

CHRISTINE. I've lied about everything ! I lied about Captain Brant ! He is Marie Brantôme's son ! And it was I he came to see, not Vinnie ! I made him come !

MANNON (*seized with fury*). You dared—— ! You—— ! The son of that—— !

CHRISTINE. Yes, I dared ! And all my trips to New York weren't to visit Father but to be with Adam ! He's gentle and tender, he's everything you've never been. He's what I've longed for all these years with you—a lover ! I love him ! So now you know the truth !

MANNON (*in a frenzy—struggling to get out of bed*). You—you whore—I'll kill you ! (*Suddenly he falls back, groaning, doubled up on his left side, with intense pain.*)

CHRISTINE (*with savage satisfaction*). Ah !

> (*She hurries through the doorway into her room and immediately returns with a small box in her hand. He is facing away from her door, and, even if the intense pain left him any perception, he could not notice her departure and return, she moves so silently.*)

MANNON (*gaspingly*). Quick—medicine !

CHRISTINE (*turned away from him, takes a pellet from the box, asking tensely as she does so*). Where is your medicine ?

MANNON. On the stand ! Hurry !

CHRISTINE. Wait. I have it now. (*She pretends to take something from the stand by the head of the bed—then holds out the pellet and a glass of water which is on the stand.*) Here. (*He turns to her, groaning, and opens his mouth. She puts the pellet on his tongue and presses the glass of water to his lips.*) Now drink.

MANNON (*takes a mouthful of water—then suddenly*

a wild look of terror comes over his face. He gasps.)
That's not—my medicine ! (*She shrinks back to
the table, the hand with the box held out behind her,
as if seeking a hiding-place. Her fingers release the
box on the table-top and she brings her hand in front
of her as if instinctively impelled to prove to him she
has nothing. His eyes are fixed on her in a terrible
accusing glare. He tries to call for help but his voice
fades to a wheezy whisper.*) Help ! Vinnie !

> (*He falls back in a coma, breathing stertorously.
> Christine stares at him, fascinated—then
> starts with terror as she hears a noise
> from the hall and frantically snatches up
> the box from the table and holds it behind
> her back, turning to face the door as it
> opens and Lavinia appears in the door-
> way. She is dressed as at the end of
> Act Three, in nightgown, wrapper and
> slippers. She stands, dazed and fright-
> ened and hesitating, as if she had just
> awakened.*)

LAVINIA. I had a horrible dream—I thought I
heard Father calling me—it woke me up——

CHRISTINE (*trembling with guilty terror—stammers*).
He just had—an attack.

LAVINIA (*hurries to the bed*). Father ! (*She puts
her arms around him.*) He's fainted !

CHRISTINE. No. He's all right now. Let him
sleep.

(*At this moment Mannon, with a last dying effort, straightens up in a sitting position in Lavinia's arms, his eyes glaring at his wife, and manages to raise his arm and point an accusing finger at her.*)

MANNON (*gasps*). She's guilty—not medicine ! (*He falls back limply.*)

LAVINIA. Father ! (*Frightened, she feels for his pulse, puts her ear against his chest to listen for a heartbeat.*)

CHRISTINE. Let him alone. He's asleep.

LAVINIA. He's dead !

CHRISTINE (*repeats mechanically*). Dead ? (*Then in a strange flat tone.*) I hope—he rests in peace.

LAVINIA (*turning on her with hatred*). Don't you dare pretend—— ! You wanted him to die ! You—— (*She stops and stares at her mother with a horrified suspicion—then harshly accusing.*) Why did he point at you like that ? Why did he say you were guilty ? Answer me !

CHRISTINE (*stammers*). I told him—Adam was my lover.

LAVINIA (*aghast*). You told him that—when you knew his heart—— ! Oh ! You did it on purpose ! You murdered him !

CHRISTINE. No—it was your fault—you made him suspicious—he kept talking of love and death——

he forced me to tell him ! (*Her voice becomes thick, as if she were drowsy and fighting off sleep. Her eyes half close.*)

LAVINIA (*grabbing her by the shoulders—fiercely*). Listen ! Look at me ! He said " not medicine " ! What did he mean ?

CHRISTINE (*keeping the hand with the poison pressed against her back*). I—I don't know.

LAVINIA. You do know ! What was it ? Tell me !

CHRISTINE (*with a last effort of will manages to draw herself up and speak with a simulation of out-raged feeling*). Are you accusing your mother of——

LAVINIA. Yes ! I—— ! (*Then distractedly.*) No—you can't be that evil !

CHRISTINE (*her strength gone—swaying weakly*). I don't know what—you're talking about. (*She edges away from Lavinia towards her bedroom door, the hand with the poison stretched out behind her—weakly.*) I—feel faint. I must go—and lie down. I—— (*She turns as if to run into the room, takes a tottering step—then her knees suddenly buckle under her and she falls in a dead faint at the foot of the bed. As her hand strikes the floor the fingers relax and the box slips out on to one of the knotted rugs. Lavinia does not notice this. Startled by Christine's collapse, she automatically bends on one knee beside her and hastily feels for her pulse. Then satisfied she has only fainted, her anguished hatred immediately returns and she speaks with strident denunciation.*) You murdered him just the same—by telling him! I suppose you think you'll be free to marry Adam now! But you won't! Not while I'm alive! I'll make you pay for your crime! I'll find a way to punish you!

> (*She is starting to her feet when her eyes fall on the little box on the rug. Immediately she snatches it up and stares at it, the look of suspicion changing to a dreadful, horrified certainty. Then with a shuddering cry she shrinks back along the side of the bed, the box clutched in her hand, and sinks on her knees by the head of the bed, and flings her arms around the dead man.*)

LAVINIA (*with anguished beseeching*). Father! Don't leave me alone! Come back to me! Tell me what to do!

(Curtain.)

The Hunted

A Play in Five Acts
Part Two of the Trilogy

Mourning Becomes Electra

Characters

CHRISTINE, *Ezra Mannon's widow.*
LAVINIA (VINNIE), *her daughter.*
ORIN, *her son, First Lieutenant of Infantry.*
CAPTAIN ADAM BRANT
HAZEL NILES
PETER, *her brother, Captain of Artillery.*
JOSIAH BORDEN, *manager of the shipping company.*
EMMA, *his wife.*
EVERETT HILLS, D.D., *of the First Congregational Church.*
HIS WIFE
DOCTOR JOSEPH BLAKE
THE CHANTYMAN

Scenes

ACT ONE

Exterior of the Mannon house—a moonlight night two days after the murder of Ezra Mannon.

ACT TWO

Sitting-room in the house (immediately follows Act One).

ACT THREE

Ezra Mannon's study (immediately follows Act Two).

ACT FOUR

The stern of the clipper ship "Flying Trades," at a wharf in East Boston—a night two days later.

ACT FIVE

Same as Act One—Exterior of the Mannon house the night of the following day.

ACT ONE

SCENE. *The same as Acts One and Three of " Homecoming "—Exterior of the Mannon House.*

*It is a moonlight night two days after the
murder of Ezra Mannon. The house has the
same strange eerie appearance, its white portico
like a mask in the moonlight, as it had on that
night. All the shutters are closed. A funeral
wreath is fixed to the column at the right of steps.
Another wreath is on the door.*

*There is a sound of voices from inside the house,
the front door is opened and Josiah Borden and
his wife, Everett Hills, the Congregational minister, and his wife, and Doctor Joseph Blake,
the Mannons' family physician, come out. Christine can be seen in the hall just inside the door.
There is a chorus of "Good night, Mrs. Mannon,"
and they turn to the steps and the door is closed.*

*These people—the Bordens, Hills and his wife
and Doctor Blake—are, as were the Ames of Act
One of " Homecoming," types of townsfolk, a
chorus representing as those others had, but in a
different stratum of society, the town as a human
background for the drama of the Mannons.*

*Josiah Borden, the manager of the Mannon
shipping company, is shrewd and competent. He
is about sixty, small and wizened, white hair
and beard, rasping nasal voice, and little sharp
eyes. His wife, about ten years his junior, is a
typical New England woman of pure English*

ancestry, with a horse face, buck teeth and big feet, her manner defensively sharp and assertive. Hills is the type of well-fed minister of a prosperous small-town congregation—stout and unctuous, snobbish and ingratiating, conscious of godliness, but timid and always feeling his way. He is in the fifties, as is his wife, a sallow, flabby, self-effacing minister's wife. Doctor Blake is the old kindly best-family physician—a stout, self-important old man with a stubborn opinionated expression.

They come down the steps to the drive. Mrs. Borden and Mrs. Hills walk together towards left front until they are by the bench. There they stop to wait for the men who stand at the foot of the steps while Borden and Blake light cigars.

MRS. BORDEN (*tartly*).   I can't abide that woman !

MRS. HILLS.   No.   There's something queer about her.

MRS. BORDEN (*grudgingly honest*).   Still and all, I come nearer to liking her now than I ever did before when I see how broken down she is over her husband's death.

MRS. HILLS.   Yes.   She looks terrible, doesn't she ?   Doctor Blake says she will have herself in bed sick if she doesn't look out.

MRS. BORDEN.   I'd never have suspected she had that much feeling in her.   Not but what she hasn't always been a dutiful wife, as far as anyone knows.

MRS. HILLS. Yes. She's seemed to be.

MRS. BORDEN. Well, it only goes to show how you can misjudge a person without meaning to— especially when that person is a Mannon. They're not easy to make head or tail of. Queer, the difference in her and Lavinia—the way they take his death. Lavinia is cold and calm as an icicle.

MRS. HILLS. Yes. She doesn't seem to feel as much sorrow as she ought.

MRS. BORDEN. That's where you're wrong. She feels it as much as her mother. Only she's too Mannon to let anyone see what she feels. But did you notice the look in her eyes?

MRS. HILLS. I noticed she never said a word to anyone. Where did she disappear to all of a sudden?

MRS. BORDEN. Went to the train with Peter Niles to meet Orin. I overheard her mother talking to Lavinia in the hall. She was insisting Peter should escort her to meet the train. Lavinia must have been starting to go alone. Her mother seemed really angry about it. (*Then glancing towards the men who have moved a little away from the steps and are standing talking in low tones.*) Whatever are those men gossiping about? (*She calls.*) Josiah! It's time we were getting home.

BORDEN. I'm coming, Emma. (*The three men join the women by the bench, Borden talking as they come*.) It isn't for me to question the arrangements she's made, Joe, but it does seem as if Ezra should have been laid out in the town hall where the whole town could have paid their respects to him, and had a big public funeral to-morrow.

HILLS. That's my opinion. He was mayor of the town and a national war hero——

BLAKE. She says it was Ezra's wish he'd often expressed that everything should be private and quiet. That's just like Ezra. He never was one for show. He did the work and let others do the showing-off.

HILLS (*unctuously*). He was a great man. His death is a real loss to everyone in this community. He was a power for good.

BORDEN. Yes. He got things done.

HILLS. What a tragedy to be taken his first night home after passing unharmed through the whole war !

BORDEN. I couldn't believe the news. Who'd ever suspect—— It's queer. It's like fate.

MRS. HILLS (*breaks in tactlessly*). Maybe it is fate. You remember, Everett, you've always said about the Mannons that pride goeth before a fall and that some day God would humble them in their sinful pride. (*Everyone stares at her, shocked and irritated.*)

HILLS (*flustered*). I don't remember ever saying——

BLAKE (*huffily*). If you'll excuse me, that's darn nonsense ! I've known Ezra Mannon all my life, and to those he wanted to know he was as plain and simple——

HILLS (*hastily*). Of course, Doctor. My wife entirely misunderstood me. I was, perhaps wrongly, referring to Mrs. Mannon.

BLAKE. She's all right too—when you get to know her.

HILLS (*dryly*). I have no doubt.

BLAKE. And it's a poor time, when this household is afflicted by sudden death, to be——

HILLS. You are quite right, Doctor. My wife should have remembered——

MRS. HILLS (*crushed*). I didn't mean anything wrong, Doctor.

BLAKE (*mollified*). Let's forget it, then. (*Turning to Borden—with a self-satisfied, knowing air.*) As for your saying who'd ever expect it—well, you and Emma know I expected Ezra wouldn't last long.

BORDEN. Yes. I remember you said you were afraid his heart was bad.

MRS. BORDEN. I remember you did too.

BLAKE. From the symptoms Mrs. Mannon described from his letter to her, I was as certain as if I'd examined him he had angina. And I wasn't surprised neither. I'd often told Ezra he was attempting more than one man could handle and if he didn't rest he'd break down. The minute they sent for me I knew what'd happened. And what she told me about waking up to find him groaning and doubled with pain confirmed it. She'd given him his medicine—it was what I would have prescribed myself—but it was too late. And as for dying his first night home—well, the war was over, he was worn out, he'd had a long, hard trip home—and angina is no respecter of time and place. It strikes when it has a mind too.

BORDEN (*shaking his head*). Too bad. Too durned bad. The town won't find another as able as Ezra in a hurry. (*They all shake their heads and look sad. A pause.*)

MRS. BORDEN. Well, we aren't doing anyone any good standing here. We ought to get home, Josiah.

MRS. HILLS. Yes. We must, too, Everett.

> (*They begin moving slowly off left, Hills going with the two women. Doctor Blake nudges Borden and motions him to stay behind. After the others disappear, he whispers with a meaning grin.*)

BLAKE. I'll tell you a secret, Josiah—strictly between you and me.

THE HUNTED

BORDEN (*sensing something from his manner—eagerly*). Of course. What is it, Joe?

BLAKE. I haven't asked Christine Mannon any embarrassing questions, but I have a strong suspicion it was love killed Ezra!

BORDEN. Love?

BLAKE. That's what! Leastways, love made angina kill him, if you take my meaning. She's a damned handsome woman and he'd been away a long time. Only natural between man and wife —but not the treatment I'd recommend for angina. He should have known better, but—well—he was human.

BORDEN (*with a salacious smirk*). Can't say as I blame him! She's handsome! I don't like her and never did, but I can imagine worse ways of dying! (*They both chuckle.*) Well, let's catch up with the folks.

> (*They go off, left. They have hardly disappeared before the door of the house is opened and Christine Mannon comes out and stands at the head of the steps a moment, then descends to the drive. She is obviously in a terrible state of strained nerves. Beneath the mask-like veneer of her face there are deep lines about her mouth, and her eyes burn with a feverish light. Feeling herself free from observa-*

tion for a moment she lets go, her mouth twitches, her eyes look desperately on all sides, as if she longed to fly from something. Hazel Niles comes out of the house to the head of the steps. She is the same as in "Homecoming." Christine at once senses her presence behind her and regains her tense control of herself.

HAZEL (*with a cheering, sympathetic air*). So here you are. I looked everywhere around the house and couldn't find you.

CHRISTINE (*tensely*). I couldn't stay in. I'm so nervous. It's been a little harrowing—all these people coming to stand around and stare at the dead—and at me.

HAZEL. I know. But there won't be any more now. (*Then a tone of eagerness breaking through in spite of herself.*) Peter and Vinnie ought to be back soon, if the train isn't late. Oh, I hope Orin will surely come!

CHRISTINE (*strangely*). The same train! It was late that night he came! Only two days ago! It seems a lifetime! I've grown old.

HAZEL (*gently*). Try not to think of it.

CHRISTINE (*tensely*). As if I hadn't tried! But my brain keeps on—over and over and over!

HAZEL. I'm so afraid you will make yourself ill.

CHRISTINE (*rallying herself and forcing a smile*). There, I'm all right. I mustn't appear too old and haggard when Orin comes, must I? He always liked me to be pretty.

HAZEL. It will be so good to see him again! (*Then quickly*). He ought to be such a comfort to you in your grief.

CHRISTINE. Yes. (*Then strangely.*) He used to be my baby, you know—before he left me. (*Suddenly staring at Hazel, as if struck by an idea.*) You love Orin, don't you?

HAZEL (*embarrassed—stammers shyly*). I—I——

CHRISTINE. I am glad. I want you to. I want him to marry you. (*Putting an arm around her—in a strained tone.*) We'll be secret conspirators, shall we, and I'll help you and you'll help me?

HAZEL. I don't understand.

CHRISTINE. You know how possessive Vinnie is with Orin. She's always been jealous of you. I warn you she'll do everything she can to keep him from marrying you.

HAZEL (*shocked*). Oh, Mrs. Mannon, I can't believe Vinnie—— !

CHRISTINE (*unheeding*). So you must help me. We mustn't let Orin come under her influence again. Especially now in the morbid, crazy state of grief she's in! Haven't you noticed how queer she's become ? She hasn't spoken a single word since her father's death ! When I talk to her she won't answer me. And yet she follows me around everywhere—she hardly leaves me alone a minute. (*Forcing a nervous laugh.*) It gets on my nerves until I could scream !

HAZEL. Poor Vinnie ! She was so fond of her father. I don't wonder she——

CHRISTINE (*staring at her—strangely*). You are genuinely good and pure of heart, aren't you ?

HAZEL (*embarrassed*). Oh no ! I'm not at all——

CHRISTINE. I was like you once—long ago—before—— (*Then with bitter longing.*) If I could only have stayed as I was then ! Why can't all of us remain innocent and loving and trusting ? But God won't leave us alone. He twists and wrings and tortures our lives with others' lives until—we poison each other to death ! (*Seeing Hazel's look, catches herself—quickly.*) Don't mind what I said ! Let's go in, shall we ? I would rather wait for Orin inside. I couldn't bear to wait and watch him coming up the drive—just like —he looks so much like his father at times—and like—but what nonsense I'm talking ! Let's go in. I hate moonlight. It makes everything so haunted.

(*She turns abruptly and goes into the house. Hazel follows her and shuts the door.*

THE HUNTED

There is a pause. Then footsteps and voices are heard from off right front and a moment later Orin Mannon enters with Peter and Lavinia. One is at once struck by his startling family resemblance to Ezra Mannon and Adam Brant (whose likeness to each other we have seen in "Homecoming"). There is the same life-like mask quality of his face in repose, the same aquiline nose, heavy eyebrows, swarthy complexion, thick straight black hair, light hazel eyes. His mouth and chin have the same general characteristics as his father's had, but the expression of his mouth gives an impression of tense oversensitiveness quite foreign to the General's, and his chin is a refined, weakened version of the dead man's. He is about the same height as Mannon and Brant, but his body is thin and his swarthy complexion sallow. He wears a bandage round his head high up on his forehead. He carries himself by turns with a marked slouchiness or with a self-conscious square-shouldered stiffness that indicates a soldierly bearing is unnatural to him. When he speaks it is jerkily, with a strange, vague, preoccupied air. But when he smiles naturally his face has a gentle boyish charm which makes women immediately want to mother him. He wears a moustache similar to Brant's which serves to increase their resemblance to each other. Although he is only twenty, he looks thirty. He is dressed in a baggy, ill-fitting uniform—that of a first lieutenant of infantry in the Union Army.)

ORIN (*as they enter looks eagerly towards the house—then with bitter, hurt disappointment in his tone*). Where's Mother? I thought she'd surely be waiting for me. (*He stands staring at the house.*) God, how I've dreamed of coming home! I thought it would never end, that we'd go on murdering and being murdered until no one was left alive! Home at last! No, by God, I must be dreaming again! (*Then in an awed tone.*) But the house looks strange. Or is it something in me? I was off my head so long, everything has seemed queer since I came back to earth. Did the house always look so ghostly and dead?

PETER. That's only the moonlight, you chump.

ORIN. Like a tomb. That's what mother used to say it reminded her of, I remember.

LAVINIA (*reproachfully*). It is a tomb—just now, Orin.

ORIN (*hurriedly—shamefacedly*). I—I'd forgotten. I simply can't realize he's dead yet. I suppose I'd come to expect he would live for ever. (*A trace of resentment has crept into his tone.*) Or, at least outlive me. I never thought his heart was weak. He told me the trouble he had wasn't serious.

LAVINIA (*quickly*). Father told you that, too ? I was hoping he had. (*Then turning to Peter.*) You go ahead in, Peter. Say we're coming a little behind. I want to speak to Orin a moment.

PETER. Sure thing, Vinnie. (*He goes in the front door, closing it behind him.*)

ORIN. I'm glad you got rid of him. Peter is all right but—I want to talk to you alone. (*With a boyish brotherly air—putting an arm around her.*) You certainly are a sight for sore eyes, Vinnie ! How are you, anyway, you old bossy fuss-buzzer ! Gosh, it seems natural to hear myself calling you that old nickname again. Aren't you glad to see me ?

LAVINIA (*affectionately*). Of course I am !

ORIN. I'd never guess it ! You've hardly spoken a word since you met me. What's happened to you ? (*Then, as she looks at him reproachfully, he takes away his arm—a bit impatiently.*) I told you I can't get used to the idea of his being dead. Forgive me, Vinnie. I know what a shock it must be to you.

LAVINIA. Isn't it a shock to you, Orin ?

ORIN. Certainly ! What do you think I am ? But—oh, I can't explain ! You wouldn't understand, unless you'd been at the front. I hardened myself to expect my own death and everyone else's, and think nothing of it. I had to—to keep alive ! It was part of my training as a soldier under him. He taught it to me, you might say ! So when it's his turn he can hardly expect—— (*He has talked with increasing bitterness. Lavinia interrupts him sharply.*)

LAVINIA. Orin ! How can you be so un-feeling ?

ORIN (*again shamefaced*). I didn't mean that. My mind is still full of ghosts. I can't grasp anything but war, in which he was so alive. He was the war to me—the war that would never end until I died. I can't understand peace—his end ! (*Then with exasperation.*) God damn it, Vinnie, give me a chance to get used to things !

LAVINIA. Orin !

ORIN (*resentfully*). I'm sorry ! Oh, I know what you're thinking ! I used to be such a nice gentlemanly cuss, didn't I ?—and now—— Well, you wanted me to be a hero in blue, so you better be resigned ! Murdering doesn't improve one's manners ! (*Abruptly changing the subject.*) But what the devil are we talking about me for ? Listen, Vinnie. There's something I want to ask you before I see Mother.

LAVINIA. Hurry, then ! She'll be coming right out ! I've got to tell you something too !

ORIN. What was that stuff you wrote about some Captain Brant coming to see Mother ? Do you mean to tell me there's actually been gossip started about her ? (*Then without waiting for a reply, bursting into jealous rage.*) By God, if he dares come here again, I'll make him damned sorry he did !

LAVINIA (*grimly*). I'm glad you feel that way about him. But there's no time to talk now. All I want to do is warn you to be on your guard. Don't let her baby you the way she used to and get you under her thumb again. Don't believe the lies she'll tell you ! Wait until you've talked to me ! Will you promise me ?

ORIN (*staring at her bewilderedly*). You mean— Mother ? (*Then angrily.*) What the hell are you talking about, anyway ? Are you loony ? Honestly, Vinnie, I call that carrying your everlasting squabble with Mother a bit too far ! You ought to be ashamed of yourself ! (*Then suspiciously.*) What are you being so mysterious about ? Is it Brant—— ?

LAVINIA (*at a sound from inside the house*). Ssshh ! (*The front door of the house is opened and Christine hurries out.*)

CHRISTINE (*angrily to Peter who is in the hall*). Why didn't you call me, Peter ? You shouldn't have left him alone ! (*She calls uncertainly :*) Orin.

ORIN. Mother ! (*She runs down the steps and flings her arms around him.*)

CHRISTINE. My boy ! My baby ! (*She kisses him.*)

ORIN (*melting, all his suspicion forgotten*). Mother ! God, it's good to see you ! (*Then almost roughly, pushing her back and staring at her.*) But you're different ! What's happened to you ?

CHRISTINE (*forcing a smile*). I ? Different ? I don't think so, dear. Certainly I hope not—to you ! (*Touching the bandage on his head—tenderly.*) Your head ! Does it pain dreadfully ? You poor darling, how you must have suffered ! (*She kisses him.*) But it's all over now, thank God. I've got you back again ! (*Keeping her arm around him, she leads him up the steps.*) Let's go in. There's someone else waiting who will be so glad to see you.

LAVINIA (*who has come to the foot of the steps— harshly*). Remember, Orin !

> (*Christine turns round to look down at her. A look of hate flashes between mother and daughter. Orin glances at his mother suspiciously and draws away from her.*)

CHRISTINE (*immediately recovers her poise—to Orin, as if Lavinia hadn't spoken*). Come on in, dear. It's chilly. Your poor head—— (*She takes his hand and leads him through the door and closes it behind them. Lavinia remains by the foot of the steps, staring after them. Then the door is suddenly opened again and Christine comes out, closing it behind her, and walks to the head of the steps. For a moment mother and daughter stare into each other's eyes. Then Christine begins haltingly in a tone she vainly tries to make kindly and persuasive.)* Vinnie, I—I must speak with you a moment—now Orin is here. I appreciate your grief has made you—not quite normal—and I make allowances. But I cannot understand your attitude towards me. Why do you keep following me everywhere—and stare at me like that ? I had been a good wife to him for twenty-three years—until I met Adam. I was guilty then, I admit. But I repented and put him out of my life. I would have been a good wife again as long as your father had lived. After all, Vinnie, I am your mother. I brought you into the world. You ought to have some feeling for me. *(She pauses, waiting for some response, but Lavinia simply stares at her, frozen and silent. Fear creeps into Christine's tone.)* Don't stare like that ! What are you thinking ? Surely you can't still have that insane suspicion—that I—— *(Then guiltily.)* What did you do that night after I fainted ? I—I've missed something—some medicine I take to put me to sleep—— *(Something like a grim smile of satisfaction forms on Lavinia's lips. Christine exclaims, frightened :)* Oh, you did—you found—and I suppose you connect that—but don't you see how insane—to suspect—when Doctor

Blake knows he died of———— ! (*Then angrily.*) I know what you've been waiting for—to tell Orin your lies and get him to go to the police ! You don't dare do that on your own responsibility— but if you can make Orin———— Isn't that it ? Isn't that what you've been planning the last two days ? Tell me ! (*Then as Lavinia remains silent, Christine gives way to fury and rushes down the steps and seizes her by the arm and shakes her.*) Answer me when I speak to you ! What are you plotting ? What are you going to do ? Tell me ! (*Lavinia keeps her body rigid, her eyes staring into her mother's. Christine lets go and steps away from her. Then Lavinia, turning her back, walks slowly and woodenly off left between the lilac clump and the house. Christine stares after her, her strength seems to leave her, she trembles with dread. From inside the house comes the sound of Orin's voice calling sharply, "Mother! Where are you ?" Christine starts and immediately by an effort of will regains control over herself. She hurries up the steps and opens the door. She speaks to Orin and her voice is tensely quiet and normal.*) Here I am, dear ! (*She shuts the door behind her.*)

(*Curtain.*)

SCENE. *The sitting-room of the Mannon house. Like
the study, but much larger, it is an interior composed
of straight severe lines with heavy detail. The
walls are plain plastered surfaces, light grey with
a white dado. It is a bleak room without intimacy,
with an atmosphere of uncomfortable, stilted state-
liness. The furniture is stationed about with exact
precision. On the left, front, is a doorway leading
to the dining-room. Further back, on the left, are
a wall table and chair and a writing desk and
chair. In the rear wall, centre, is the doorway
giving on the main hall and the stairs. At right
is a fireplace with a chimney-piece of black marble,
flanked by two windows. Portraits of ancestors
hang on the walls. At the rear of the fireplace,
on the right, is one of a grim-visaged minister
of the witch-burning era. Between fireplace and
front is another of Ezra Mannon's grandfather,
in the uniform of an officer in Washington's army.
Directly over the fireplace is the portrait of Ezra's
father, Abe Mannon, done when he was sixty.
Except for the difference in ages, his face looks
exactly like Ezra's in the painting in the study.*

*Of the three portraits on the other walls, two
are of women—Abe Mannon's wife and the wife
of Washington's officer. The third has the appearance of a prosperous shipowner of Colonial days.
All the faces in the portraits have the same mask
quality of those of the living characters in the play.*

At the left centre of the room, front, is a table with two chairs. There is another chair at centre, front, and a sofa at right, front, facing left.

The opening of this scene follows immediately the close of the preceding one. Hazel is discovered sitting on the chair at centre, front. Peter is sitting on the sofa at right. From the hall Orin is heard calling, "Mother! Where are you?" as at the close of the preceding act.

HAZEL. Where can she have gone? She's worked herself into such a state of grief I don't think she knows what she's doing.

PETER. Vinnie's completely knocked out, too.

HAZEL. And poor Orin! What a terrible homecoming this is for him! How ill and changed he looks, doesn't he, Peter?

PETER. Head wounds are no joke. He's darned lucky to have come out alive.

> *(They self-consciously stop talking as Orin and Christine enter from the rear. Orin is questioning her suspiciously.)*

ORIN. Why did you sneak away like that? What were you doing?

CHRISTINE (*forcing a wan smile*). The happiness of seeing you again was a little too much for me, I'm afraid, dear. I suddenly felt as if I were going to faint, so I rushed out in the fresh air.

ORIN (*immediately ashamed of himself—tenderly, putting his arm around her*). Poor Mother ! I'm sorry—— Look here, then. You sit down and rest. Or maybe you better go right to bed.

HAZEL. That's right, Orin, you make her. I've been trying to get her to but she won't listen to me.

CHRISTINE. Go to bed the minute he comes home ! I should say not !

ORIN (*worried and pleased at the same time*). But you mustn't do anything to——

CHRISTINE (*patting his cheek*). Fiddlesticks ! Having you again is just the medicine I need to give me strength—to bear things. (*She turns to Hazel.*) Listen to him, Hazel ! You'd think I was the invalid and not he.

HAZEL. Yes. You've got to take care of yourself, too, Orin.

ORIN. Oh, forget me. I'm all right.

CHRISTINE. We'll play nurses, Hazel and I, and have you your old self again before you know it. Won't we, Hazel ?

HAZEL (*smiling happily*). Of course we will.

CHRISTINE. Don't stand, dear. You must be worn out. Wait. We'll make you comfortable. Hazel, will you bring me a cushion ?

(*Hazel gets a cushion and helps to place it behind his back in the chair at right of table. Orin's eyes light up and he grins boyishly, obviously revelling in being coddled.*)

ORIN. How's this for the comforts of home, Peter ? The front was never like this, eh ?

PETER. Not so you'd notice it !

ORIN (*with a wink at Hazel*). Peter will be getting jealous ! You better call Vinnie in to put a pillow behind him !

HAZEL (*with a smile*). I can't picture Vinnie being that soft.

ORIN (*a jealous resentment creeping into his voice.*) She can be soft—on occasion. She's always coddling Father and he likes it, although he pretends——

CHRISTINE (*turning away and restraining a shudder*). Orin ! You're talking as if he were—alive !

(*There is an uncomfortable silence. Hazel goes quietly back to her chair at centre. Christine goes round the table to the chair opposite Orin and sits down.*)

ORIN (*with a wry smile*). We'd all forgotten he's dead, hadn't we ? Well, I can't believe it even yet. I feel him in this house—alive !

CHRISTINE. Orin !

ORIN (*strangely*). Everything is changed—in some queer way—this house, Vinnie, you, I—everything but Father. He's the same and always will be—here—the same ! Don't you feel that, Mother ? (*She shivers, looking before her, but doesn't answer*).

HAZEL (*gently*). You mustn't make your mother think of it, Orin.

ORIN (*staring at her—in a queer tone of gratitude*). You're the same, Hazel—sweet and good. (*He turns to his mother accusingly.*) At least Hazel hasn't changed, thank God !

CHRISTINE (*rousing herself—turns to force a smile at him*). Hazel will never change, I hope. I am glad you appreciate her. (*Hazel looks embarrassed. Christine goes on—with motherly solicitude.*) Wasn't the long train trip terribly hard on you, dear ?

ORIN. Well, it wasn't a pleasure trip exactly. My head got aching till I thought it would explode.

CHRISTINE (*leans over and puts her hand on his forehead*). Poor boy ! Does it pain now ?

ORIN. Not much. Not at all when your hand is there. (*Impulsively he takes her hand and kisses it—boyishly.*) Gosh, Mother, it feels so darned good to be home with you ! (*Then staring at her suspiciously again.*) Let me have a good look at you. You're so different. I noticed it even outside. What is it ?

CHRISTINE (*avoiding his eyes—forcing a smile*). It's just that I'm getting old, I'm afraid, dear.

ORIN. No. You're more beautiful than ever ! You're younger, too, somehow. But it isn't that. (*Almost pushing her hand away—bitterly.*) Maybe I can guess !

CHRISTINE (*forces a laugh*). Younger and more beautiful ! Do you hear him going on, Hazel ? He has learned to be very gallant, I must say !

> (*Lavinia appears in the doorway at rear. She enters but remains standing just inside the doorway and keeps her eyes fixed on her mother and Orin.*)

ORIN (*who is again looking at Hazel, breaks out harshly*). Do you remember how you waved your handkerchief, Hazel, the day I set off to become a hero ? I thought you would sprain your wrist ! And all the mothers and wives and sisters and girls did the same ! Some time in some war they ought to make the women take the men's place for a month or so. Give them a taste of murder !

CHRISTINE. Orin !

ORIN. Let them batter each other's brains out with rifle butts and rip each other's guts with bayonets ! After that, maybe they'd stop waving handkerchiefs and chattering about heroes ! (*Hazel gives a shocked exclamation.*)

CHRISTINE. Please !

PETER (*gruffly*). Give it a rest, Orin ! It's over. Give yourself a chance to forget it. None of us liked it any more than you did.

ORIN (*immediately shamefaced*). You're right, Peter. I'm a damned whining fool ! I'm sorry, Hazel. That was rotten of me.

HAZEL. It was nothing, Orin. I understand how you feel. Really I do.

ORIN. I—I let off steam when I shouldn't. (*Then suddenly.*) Do you still sing, Hazel ? I used to hear you singing—down there. It made me feel life might still be alive somewhere—that, and my dreams of Mother, and the memory of Vinnie bossing me around like a drill sergeant. I used to hear you singing at the queerest times—so sweet and clear and pure ! It would rise above the screams of the dying——

CHRISTINE (*tensely*). I wish you wouldn't talk of death !

LAVINIA (*from the doorway—in a brusque commanding tone like her father's*). Orin ! Come and see Father.

ORIN (*starts up from his chair and makes an automatic motion as if to salute—mechanically*). Yes, sir. (*Then confusedly.*) What the devil—— ? You sounded just like him. Don't do that again, for heaven's sake ! (*He tries to force a laugh—then shamefacedly*.) I meant to look at him the first thing—but I got talking—I'll go in now.

CHRISTINE (*her voice tense and strained*). No! Wait! (*Angrily to Lavinia*.) Can't you let your brother have a minute to rest? You can see how worn out he is! (*Then to Orin*.) I've hardly had a chance to say a word to you yet—and it has been so long! Stay with me a little while, won't you?

ORIN (*touched, coming back to her*). Of course, Mother! You come before everything!

LAVINIA (*starts to make a bitter retort, glances at Peter and Hazel, then remarks evenly*). Very well. Only remember what I said, Orin. (*She turns her back and starts to go into the hall*.)

CHRISTINE (*frightened*). Vinnie! Where are you going?

LAVINIA (*does not answer her but calls back to her brother over her shoulder*). You'll come in a little while, won't you?

> (*She disappears across the hall. Orin gives his mother a sidelong glance of uneasy suspicion. Christine is desperately trying to appear calm. Peter and Hazel stand up, feeling uncomfortable*.)

HAZEL. Peter, we really must be getting home.

PETER. Yes.

CHRISTINE. It was so kind of you to come.

HAZEL (*giving her hand to Orin*). You must rest all you can now, Orin—and try not to think about things.

ORIN. You're darned kind, Hazel. It's fine to see you again—the same as ever !

HAZEL (*delighted but pulling her hand away shyly*). I'm glad, too. Good night, Orin.

PETER (*shakes his hand*). Good night. Rest and take it easy.

ORIN. Good night, Peter. Thanks for meeting me.

CHRISTINE (*goes with them to the hall.*) I'm afraid this isn't a very cheerful house to visit just now —but please come soon again. You will do Orin more good than anyone, Hazel.

> (*The look of suspicion again comes to Orin's eyes. He sits down in the chair at left of table and stares before him bitterly. Christine returns from the hall, closing the sliding doors behind her silently. She stands for a moment looking at Orin, visibly bracing herself for the ordeal of the coming interview, her eyes full of tense calculating fear.*)

ORIN (*without looking at her*). What's made you take such a fancy to Hazel all of a sudden ? You never used to think much of her. You didn't want me going about with her.

CHRISTINE (*coming forward and sitting across the table from him—in her gentle motherly tone*). I was selfish then. I was jealous, too, I'll confess. But all I want now is your happiness, dear. I know how much you used to like Hazel——

ORIN (*blurts out*). That was only to make you jealous ! (*Then bitterly.*) But now you're a widow, I'm not home an hour before you're trying to marry me off ! You must be damned anxious to get rid of me again ! Why ?

CHRISTINE. You mustn't say that ! If you knew how horribly lonely I've been without you——

ORIN. So lonely you've written me exactly two letters in the last six months !

CHRISTINE. But I wrote you many more ! They must have been lost——

ORIN. I received all of Hazel's letters—and Vinnie's. It's darned funny yours should be the only ones to get lost ! (*Unable to hold back any longer, he bursts forth*). Who is this Captain Brant who's been calling on you ?

CHRISTINE (*prepared for this—with well-feigned astonishment*). On me ? You mean on Vinnie, don't you ? (*Then as Orin looks taken aback.*) Wherever did you get that silly idea ? Oh, of course, I know ! Vinnie must have written you the same nonsense she did to your father.

ORIN. She wrote it to him ? What did he do ?

CHRISTINE. Why, he laughed at it, naturally ! Your father was very fond of Vinnie but he knew how jealous she's always been of me and he realized she'd tell any lie she could to——

ORIN. Oh, come on now, Mother ! Just because you're always getting on each other's nerves it doesn't mean Vinnie would ever deliberately——

CHRISTINE. Oh, doesn't it though ? I think you'll discover before you're much older that there isn't anything your sister will stop at—that she will even accuse me of the vilest, most horrible things !

ORIN. Mother ! Honestly now ! You oughtn't to say that !

CHRISTINE (*reaching out and taking his hand*). I mean it, Orin. I wouldn't say it to anyone but you. You know that. But we've always been so close, you and I. I feel you are really—my flesh and blood ! She isn't ! She is your father's ! You're a part of me !

ORIN (*with strange eagerness*). Yes ! I feel that, too, Mother !

CHRISTINE. I know I can trust you to understand now as you always used to. (*With a tender smile.*) We had a secret little world of our own in the old days, hadn't we ?—which no one but us knew about.

ORIN (*happily*). You bet we did ! No Mannons allowed was our password, remember !

CHRISTINE. And that's what your father and Vinnie could never forgive us ! But we'll make that little world of our own again, won't we ?

ORIN. Yes !

CHRISTINE. I want to make up to you for all the injustice you suffered at your father's hands. It may seem a hard thing to say about the dead, but he was jealous of you. He hated you because he knew I loved you better than anything in the world !

ORIN (*pressing her hand in both of his—intensely*). Do you, Mother ? Do you honestly ? (*Then he is struck by what she said about his father—painfully.*) I knew he disapproved of me. But I never thought he went as far as to—hate me.

CHRISTINE. He did, just the same !

ORIN (*with resentful bitterness*). All right then ! I'll tell you the truth, Mother. I won't pretend to you I'm sorry he's dead !

CHRISTINE (*lowering her voice to a whisper*). Yes. I am glad, too !—that he has left us alone ! Oh, how happy we'll be together, you and I, if you only won't let Vinnie poison your mind against me with her disgusting lies !

ORIN (*immediately uneasy again*). What lies ? (*He releases her hand and stares at her, morbidly suspicious.*) You haven't told me about that Brant yet.

CHRISTINE. There's nothing to tell—except in Vinnie's morbid revengeful mind! I tell you, Orin, you can't realize how she's changed while you've been away! She's always been a moody and strange girl, you know that, but since you've gone she has worried and brooded until I really believe she went a little out of her mind. She got so she'd say the most terrible things about everyone. You simply wouldn't believe me, if I told you some of the things. And now, with the shock of your father's death on top of everything, I'm convinced she's actually insane. Haven't you noticed how queerly she acts? You must have!

ORIN. I saw she'd changed a lot. She seemed strange. But——

CHRISTINE. And her craziness all works out in hatred for me! Take this Captain Brant affair, for example——

ORIN. Ah!

CHRISTINE. A stupid ship's captain I happened to meet at your grandfather's who took it into his silly head to call here a few times without being asked. Vinnie thought he was coming to court her. I honestly believe she fell in love with him, Orin. But she soon discovered that he wasn't after her at all!

ORIN. Who was he after—you?

CHRISTINE (sharply). Orin! I'd be very angry

143

with you if it weren't so ridiculous ! (*She forces a laugh.*) You don't seem to realize I'm an old married woman with two grown-up children ! No, all he was after was to insinuate himself as a family friend and use your father when he came home to get him a better ship ! I soon saw through his little scheme and he'll never call here again, I promise you that ! (*She laughs—then with a teasing air.*) And that's the whole of the great Captain Brant scandal ! Are you satisfied now, you jealous goose, you ?

ORIN (*penitent and happy*). I'm a fool ! The war has got me silly, I guess ! If you knew all the hell I've been through !

CHRISTINE. It was Vinnie's fault you ever went to war ! I'll never forgive her for that ! It broke my heart, Orin ! (*Then quickly.*) But I was going to give you an example of her insane suspicions from the Captain Brant incident. Would you believe it that she has worked it all out that because his name is Brant, he must be the son of that nurse girl Marie Brantôme ? Isn't that crazy ? And to imagine for a moment, if he were, he'd ever come here to visit !

ORIN (*his face hardening*). By God, I'd like to see him ! His mother brought disgrace enough on our family without——

CHRISTINE (*frightened, shrinking from him*). Orin ! Don't look like that ! You're so like your father !

(*Then hurrying on.*) But I haven't told you the worst yet. Vinnie actually accuses me—your mother—of being in love with that fool and of having met him in New York and gone to his room ! I am no better than a prostitute in your sister's eyes !

ORIN (*stunned*). I don't believe it ! Vinnie couldn't !

CHRISTINE. I told you she'd gone crazy ! She even followed me to New York, when I went to see your sick grandfather, to spy on me. She saw me meet a man—and immediately to her crazy brain the man was Brant. Oh, it's too revolting, Orin ! You don't know what I've had to put up with from Vinnie, or you'd pity me !

ORIN. Good God ! Did she tell Father that ? No wonder he's dead ! (*Then harshly.*) Who was this man you met in New York ?

CHRISTINE. It was Mr. Lamar, your grandfather's old friend who has known me ever since I was a baby ! I happened to meet him and he asked me to go with him to call on his daughter. (*Then, seeing Orin wavering, pitifully.*) Oh, Orin ! You pretend to love me ! And yet you question me as if you suspected me, too ! And you haven't Vinnie's excuse ! You aren't out of your mind ! (*She weeps hysterically.*)

ORIN (*overcome at once by remorse and love*). No ! I swear to you ! (*He throws himself on his knees*

beside her and puts his arm around her.) Mother !
Please ! Don't cry ! I do love you ! I do !

CHRISTINE. I haven't told you the most horrible
thing of all ! Vinnie suspects me of having
poisoned your father !

ORIN (*horrified*). What ! No, by God, that's
too much ! If that's true, she ought to be put in
an asylum !

CHRISTINE. She found some medicine I take to
make me sleep, but she is so crazy I know she thinks
———— (*Then, with real terror, clinging to him.*) Oh,
Orin, I'm so afraid of her ! God knows what she
might do, in her state ! She might even go to the
police and——— Don't let her turn you against
me ! Remember you're all I have to protect me !
You are all I have in the world, dear !

ORIN (*tenderly soothing her*). Turn me against
you ? She can't be so crazy as to try that ! But
listen. I honestly think you——— You're a little
hysterical, you know. That—about Father—is all
such damned nonsense ! And as for her going to
the police—do you suppose I wouldn't prevent that
—for a hundred reasons—the family's sake—my
own sake and Vinnie's, too, as well as yours—even
if I knew———

CHRISTINE (*staring at him—in a whisper*). Knew ?
Orin, you don't believe——— ?

ORIN. No ! For God's sake ! I only meant

that no matter what you ever did, I love you better than anything in the world and——

CHRISTINE (*in an outburst of grateful joy—pressing him to her and kissing him*). Oh, Orin, you are my boy, my baby ! I love you !

ORIN. Mother ! (*Then seizing her by the shoulders and staring into her eyes—with sombre intensity.*) I could forgive anything—anything !—in my mother—except that other—that about Brant !

CHRISTINE. I swear to you—— !

ORIN. If I thought that damned—— ! (*With savage vengefulness.*) By God, I'd show you then I hadn't been taught to kill for nothing !

CHRISTINE (*full of new terror now—for Brant's life —distractedly*). For God's sake, don't talk like that ! You're not like my Orin ! You're cruel and horrible ! You frighten me !

ORIN (*immediately contrite and soothing, petting her*). There, there, Mother ! We won't ever think about it again ! We'll talk of something else. I want to tell you something. (*He sits on the floor at her feet and looks up into her face. A pause. Then he asks tenderly, taking her hand.*) Did you really want me to come back, Mother ?

CHRISTINE (*has calmed herself, but her eyes are still terrified and her voice trembles*). What a foolish question, dear.

ORIN. But your letters got farther and farther between—and they seemed so cold ! It drove me crazy ! I wanted to desert and run home—or else get killed ! If you only knew how I longed to be here with you—like this ! (*He leans his head against her knee. His voice becomes dreamy and low and caressing.*) I used to have the most wonderful dreams about you. Have you ever read a book called " Typee "—about the South Sea Islands ?

CHRISTINE (*with a start—strangely*). Islands ! Where there is peace ?

ORIN. Then you did read it ?

CHRISTINE. No.

ORIN. Someone lent me the book. I read it and re-read it until finally those Islands came to mean everything that wasn't war, everything that was peace and warmth and security. I used to dream I was there. And later on all the time I was out of my mind I seemed really to be there. There was no one there but you and me. And yet I never saw you, that's the funny part. I only felt you all around me. The breaking of the waves was your voice. The sky was the same colour as your eyes. The warm sand was like your skin. The whole island was you. (*He smiles with a dreamy tenderness.*) A strange notion, wasn't it ? But you needn't be provoked at being an island because this was the most beautiful island in the world—as beautiful as you, Mother !

THE HUNTED

CHRISTINE (*has been staring over his head, listening fascinatedly, more and more deeply moved. As he stops, an agonizing tenderness for him wells up in her —with tortured longing*). Oh, if only you had never gone away ! If you only hadn't let them take you from me !

ORIN (*uneasily*). But I've come back. Everything is all right now, isn't it ?

CHRISTINE (*hastily*). Yes ! I didn't mean that. It had to be.

ORIN. And I'll never leave you again now. I don't want Hazel or anyone. (*With a tender grin.*) You're my only girl !

CHRISTINE (*again with tenderness, stroking his hair —smiling*). You're a big man now, aren't you ? I can't believe it. It seems only yesterday when I used to find you in your nightshirt hiding in the hall upstairs on the chance that I'd come up and you'd get one more good-night kiss ! Do you remember ?

ORIN (*with a boyish grin*). You bet I remember ! And what a row there was when Father caught me ! And do you remember how you used to let me brush your hair and how I loved to ? He hated me doing that, too. You've still got the same beautiful hair, Mother. That hasn't changed. (*He reaches up and touches her hair caressingly. She gives a little shudder of repulsion and draws away from him but he*

149

is too happy to notice.) Oh, Mother, it's going to be wonderful from now on ! We'll get Vinnie to marry Peter and there will be just you and I ! (*The sliding doors in rear are opened a little and Lavinia slips silently in and stands looking at them.*)

CHRISTINE (*immediately senses her presence—controlling a start, harshly*). What do you want ? (*Orin turns to look at his sister resentfully.*)

LAVINIA (*in a flat, emotionless voice*). Aren't you coming in to see Father, Orin ?

ORIN (*scrambling to his feet—irritably*). Oh, all right, I'll come now.

> (*He hurries out past Lavinia with the air of one with a disagreeable duty he wants to get over quickly, and closes the door with a bang behind him. Lavinia stares at her mother a moment—then about-faces stiffly to follow him.*)

CHRISTINE (*springs to her feet*). Vinnie ! (*As Lavinia turns to face her—sharply.*) Come here— please. I don't want to shout across the room. (*Lavinia comes slowly forward until she is at arm's length. Her eyes grow bleak and her mouth tightens to a thin line. The resemblance between mother and daughter as they stand confronting each other is strikingly brought out. Christine begins to speak in a low voice, coolly defiant, almost triumphant.*) Well, you can go ahead now and tell Orin anything you wish ! I've already told him—so you might as well save

yourself the trouble. He said you must be insane !
I told him how you lied about my trips to New
York—for revenge !—because you loved Adam
yourself ! (*Lavinia makes a movement like a faint
shudder but is immediately stiff and frozen again.
Christine smiles tauntingly.*) So hadn't you better
leave Orin out of it ? You can't get him to go to
the police for you. Even if you convinced him I
poisoned your father, you couldn't ! He doesn't
want—any more than you do, or your father, or
any of the Mannon dead—such a public disgrace
as a murder trial would be ! For it would all come
out ! Everything ! Who Adam is and my adultery and your knowledge of it—and your love for
Adam ! Oh, believe me, I'll see to it that comes
out if anything ever gets to a trial ! I'll show you
to the world as a daughter who desired her mother's
lover and then tried to get her mother hanged out
of hatred and jealousy ! (*She laughs tauntingly.
Lavinia is trembling but her face remains hard and
emotionless. Her lips open as if to speak but she closes
them again. Christine seems drunk with her own
defiant recklessness.*) Go on ! Try and convince
Orin of my wickedness ! He loves me ! He
hated his father ! He's glad he's dead ! Even if
he knew I had killed him, he'd protect me ! (*Then
all her defiant attitude collapses and she pleads, seized
by an hysterical terror, by some fear she has kept hidden.*)
For God's sake, keep Orin out of this ! He's
still ill ! He's changed ! He's grown hard and
cruel ! All he thinks of is death ! Don't tell him

about Adam ! He would kill him ! I couldn't live then ! I would kill myself ! (*Lavinia starts and her eyes light up with a cruel hatred. Again her pale lips part as if she were about to say something, but she controls the impulse and turns away abruptly and walks with jerky steps from the room like some tragic mechanical doll. Christine stares after her—then as she disappears, collapses, catching at the table for support—in terror.*) I've got to see Adam ! I've got to warn him ! (*She sinks in the chair at right of table.*)

(*Curtain.*)

ACT THREE

SCENE. *The same as Act Two of " Homecoming "—*
Ezra Mannon's study. His body, dressed in full
uniform, is laid out on a bier draped in black
which is placed lengthwise directly below the
portrait of him over the fireplace. His head is
to right. His mask-like face is a startling repro-
duction of the face in the portrait above him, but
grimly remote and austere in death, like the carven
face of a statue.

The table and chairs which had been at centre
have been moved to the left. There is a lamp
on this table. Two stands of three lighted candles
are at each end of the black marble chimneypiece,
throwing their light above on the portrait and
below on the dead man. There is a chair by the
dead man's head, at front of bier.

Orin is standing by the head of the bier, at the
rear of it, stiffly erect like a sentinel at attention.
He is not looking down at his father but is staring
straight before him, deep in suspicious brooding.
His face in the candlelight bears a striking resem-
blance to that of the portrait above him and the
dead man's.

The time of the opening of this act precedes by
a few moments that of the end of the previous
act.

ORIN (*ashamed and guilty—bursts out angrily at*
himself). Christ, I won't have such thoughts !   I

am a rotten swine to—— Damn Vinnie! She must be crazy! (*Then, as if to distract his mind from these reflections, he turns to gaze down at his father. At the same moment Lavinia appears silently in the doorway from the hall and stands looking at him. He does not notice her entrance. He stares at his father's mask-like face and addresses it with a strange friendly mockery.*) Who are you? Another corpse! You and I have seen fields and hillsides sown with them—and they meant nothing!—nothing but a dirty joke life plays on life! (*Then with a dry smile.*) Death sits so naturally on you! Death becomes the Mannons! You were always like the statue of an eminent dead man—sitting on a chair in a park or straddling a horse in a town square— looking over the head of life without a sign of recognition—cutting it dead for the impropriety of living! (*He chuckles to himself with a queer affectionate amusement.*) You never cared to know me in life—but I really think we might be friends now you are dead!

LAVINIA (*sternly*). Orin!

ORIN (*turns to her startledly*). Damn it, don't sneak around like that! What are you trying to do, anyway? I'm jumpy enough without—— (*Then as she turns and locks the door behind her— suspiciously.*) What are you locking the door for?

LAVINIA. I've got to talk to you—and I don't want to be interrupted. (*Then sternly.*) What made you say such things just then ? I wouldn't believe you could have grown so callous to all feeling of respect——

ORIN (*guilty and resentful*). You folks at home take death so solemnly ! You would have soon learned at the front that it's only a joke ! You don't understand, Vinnie. You have to learn to mock or go crazy, can't you see ? I didn't mean it in an unkind way. It simply struck me he looks so strangely familiar—the same familiar stranger I've never known. (*Then glancing at the dead man with a kindly amused smile.*) Do you know his nickname in the army ? Old Stick—short for Stick-in-the-Mud. Grant himself started it—said Father was no good on an offensive but he'd trust him to stick in the mud and hold a position until hell froze over !

LAVINIA. Orin ! Don't you realize he was your father and he is dead ?

ORIN (*irritably*). What Grant said was a big compliment in a way.

LAVINIA. When I think of how proud of you he was when he came home ! He boasted that you had done one of the bravest things he'd seen in the war !

ORIN (*astonished—then grins with bitter mockery*). One of the bravest things he'd seen ! Oh, that's too rich ! I'll tell you the joke about that heroic deed. It really began the night before when I sneaked through their lines. I was always volunteering for extra danger. I was so scared anyone would guess I was afraid ! There was a thick mist and it was so still you could hear the fog seeping into the ground. I met a Reb crawling towards our lines. His face drifted out of the mist towards mine. I shortened my sword and let him have the point under the ear. He stared at me with an idiotic look as if he'd sat on a tack—and his eyes dimmed and went out—— (*His voice has sunk lower and lower, as if he were talking to himself. He pauses and stares over his father's body fascinatedly at nothing.*)

LAVINIA (*with a shudder*). Don't think of that now !

ORIN (*goes on with the same air*). Before I'd got back I had to kill another in the same way. It was like murdering the same man twice. I had a queer feeling that war meant murdering the same man over and over, and that in the end I would discover the man was myself ! Their faces keep coming back in dreams—and they change to Father's face—or to mine—— What does that mean, Vinnie ?

LAVINIA. I don't know ! I've got to talk to you ! For heaven's sake forget the war ! It's over now !

ORIN. Not inside us who killed ! (*Then quickly*

—*with a bitter, joking tone.*) The rest is all a joke! The next morning I was in the trenches. This was at Petersburg. I hadn't slept. My head was queer. I thought what a joke it would be on the stupid Generals like Father if everyone on both sides suddenly saw the joke war was on them and laughed and shook hands! So I began to laugh and walked towards their lines with my hand out. Of course, the joke was on me and I got this wound in the head for my pains. I went mad, wanted to kill, and ran on, yelling. Then a lot of our fools went crazy too, and followed me, and we captured a part of their line we hadn't dared tackle before. I had acted without orders, of course—but Father decided it was better policy to overlook that and let me be a hero! So do you wonder I laugh?

LAVINIA (*soothingly, coming to him and taking his arm*). You were brave and you know it. I'm proud of you, too.

ORIN (*helplessly*). Oh, all right! Be proud, then! (*He leaves her and sprawls in the chair at left of table. She stands by the head of the bier and faces him. He says resentfully:*) Well? Fire away and let's get this over! But you're wasting your breath. I know what you're going to say. Mother warned me. (*The whole memory of what his mother had said rushes over him.*) My God, how can you think such things of Mother? What the hell's got into you? (*Then humouringly.*) But I realize you're not yourself. I know how hard his death has hit you. Don't you think it would be better to postpone our talk until——

LAVINIA. No ! (*Bitterly*). Has she succeeded in convincing you I'm out of my mind ? Oh, Orin, how can you be so stupid ? (*She goes to him and, grasping him by his shoulders, brings her face close to him—compellingly.*) Look at me ! You know in your heart I'm the same as I always was—your sister—who loves you, Orin !

ORIN (*moved*). I didn't mean—I only think the shock of his death——

LAVINIA. I've never lied to you, have I ? Even when we were little you always knew I told you the truth, didn't you ?

ORIN. Yes—but——

LAVINIA. Then you must believe I wouldn't lie to you now !

ORIN. No one is saying you'd deliberately lie. It's a question of——

LAVINIA. And even if she's got you so under her thumb again that you doubt my word, you can't doubt the absolute proof !

ORIN (*roughly*). Never mind what you call proofs ! I know all about them already ! (*Then excitedly.*) Now, listen here, if you think you're going to tell me a lot of crazy stuff about Mother,

I warn you I won't listen ! So shut up before you start !

LAVINIA (*threateningly now*). If you don't, I'll go to the police !

ORIN. Don't be a damn fool !

LAVINIA. As a last resort I will—if you force me to !

ORIN. By God, you must be crazy even to talk of—— !

LAVINIA. They won't think so !

ORIN. Vinnie ! Do you realize what it would mean—— ?

LAVINIA. I realize only too well ! You and I, who are innocent, would suffer a worse punishment than the guilty—for we'd have to live on ! It would mean that Father's memory and that of all the honourable Mannon dead would be dragged through the horror of a murder trial ! But I'd rather suffer that than let the murder of our father go unpunished !

ORIN. Good God, do you actually believe—— ?

LAVINIA. Yes ! I accuse her of murder ! (*She takes the little box she has found in Christine's room soon after the murder [Act Four " Homecoming "] from the bosom of her dress and holds it out to him.*) You see this ? I found it just after Father died !

159

ORIN. Don't be a damned lunatic ! She told me all about that ! It's only some stuff she takes to make her sleep !

LAVINIA (*goes on implacably, ignoring his interruptions*). And Father knew she'd poisoned him ! He said to me, " She's guilty ! "

ORIN. That's all your crazy imagination ! God, how can you think—— ? Do you realize you're deliberately accusing your own mother—— It's too horrible and mad ! I'll have you declared insane by Doctor Blake and put away in an asylum !

LAVINIA. I swear by our dead father I am telling you the truth ! (*She puts her hand on the dead man and addresses him.*) Make Orin believe me, Father !

ORIN (*harshly*). Don't drag him in ! He always sided with you against Mother and me ! (*He grabs her arm and forces the box from her hand.*) Here ! Give me that ! (*He slips it into his coat pocket.*)

LAVINIA. Ah ! So you are afraid it's true !

ORIN. No ! But I'm going to stop your damned—— But I'm a fool to pay any attention to you ! The whole thing is too insane ! I won't talk to a crazy woman ! But, by God, you look out, Vinnie ! You leave Mother alone or—— !

LAVINIA (*regarding him bitterly*). Poor Father ! He thought the war had made a man of you ! But you're not ! You're still the spoiled cry-baby that she can make a fool of whenever she pleases !

ORIN (*stung*). That's enough from you !

LAVINIA. Oh, she warned me just now what to expect ! She boasted that you wouldn't believe me, and that even if you knew she'd murdered Father you would be glad because you hated him ! (*Then a note of entreaty in her voice.*) Orin ! For God's sake—here, before him !—tell me that isn't true, at least !

ORIN (*overcome by a sense of guilt—violently defensive*). Of course, I never said that—and I don't believe she did. But Mother means a thousand times more to me than he ever did ! I say that before him now as I would if he could hear me !

LAVINIA (*with a calculated scornful contempt now*). Then if I can't make you see your duty one way, I will another ! If you won't help me punish her, I hope you're not such a coward that you're willing to let her lover escape !

ORIN (*in a tone of awakening suspicion*). Lover ? Who do you mean ?

LAVINIA. I mean the man who plotted Father's murder with her, who must have got the poison for her ! I mean the Captain Brant I wrote you about !

ORIN (*thickly, trying to fight back his jealous sus-*

picion).   You lie !   She told me your rotten lies—about him—about following her to New York. That was Mr. Lamar she met.

LAVINIA.   So that's what she told you !   As if I could mistake Lamar for Adam Brant !   What a fool you are, Orin !   She kisses you and pretends she loves you—when she'd forgotten you were ever alive, when all she's thought of is this low lover of hers—— !

ORIN (*wildly*).   Stop !   I won't stand—— !

LAVINIA.   When all she is thinking of even now is how she can use you to keep me from doing anything, so she'll get a chance to run off and marry him !

ORIN.   You lie !

LAVINIA.   She pets you and plays the loving mother and you're so blind you can't see through her !   I tell you she went to his room !   I followed them upstairs.   I heard her telling him, " I love you, Adam."   She was kissing him !

ORIN (*takes her by the shoulder and shakes her, forcing her to her knees—frenziedly*).   Damn you ! Tell me you're lying or—— !

LAVINIA (*unafraid—looking up into his eyes—coldly*).   You know I'm not lying !   She's been going to New York on the excuse of visiting Grandfather Hamel, but really to give herself to—— !

ORIN (*in anguish*). You lie, damn you !
(*Threateningly.*) You dare say that about Mother !
Now you've got to prove it or else——— ! You're
not insane ! You know what you're saying ! So
you prove it—or by God, I'll——— !

LAVINIA (*taking his hands off her shoulders and
rising*). All I ask is a chance to prove it ! (*Then
intensely.*) But when I do, will you help me punish
Father's murderers ?

ORIN (*in a burst of murderous rage*). I'll kill that
bastard ! (*In anguished uncertainty again.*) But
you haven't proved anything yet ! It's only your
word against hers ! I don't believe you ! You
say Brant is her lover ! If that's true, I'll hate
her ! I'll know she murdered Father then ! I'll
help you punish her ! But you've got to prove it !

LAVINIA (*coldly*). I can do that very soon. She's
frightened out of her wits ! She'll go to see Brant
the first chance she gets. We must give her that
chance. Will you believe me when you find them
together ?

ORIN (*tortured*). Yes. (*Then in a burst of rage.*)
God damn him, I'll——— !

LAVINIA (*sharply*). Ssshh ! Be quiet. There's
someone in the hall ! (*They wait, staring at the
door. Then someone knocks loudly.*)

CHRISTINE (*her voice comes through the door,
frightened and strained*). Orin !

ORIN (*stammers*).   God !   I can't face her now !

LAVINIA (*in a quick whisper*).   Don't let her know you suspect her.   Pretend you think I'm out of my mind, as she wanted you to.

CHRISTINE.   Orin !   Why don't you answer me ?   (*She tries the doorknob, and finding the door locked, her voice becomes terrified.*)   Why have you locked me out ?   Let me in !   (*She pounds on the door violently.*)

LAVINIA (*in a whisper*).   Answer her.   Let her in.

ORIN (*obeying mechanically—calls in a choked voice*). All right.   I'm coming. (*He moves reluctantly towards the door.*)

LAVINIA (*struck by a sudden idea—grasps his arm*). Wait !   (*Before he can prevent it, she reaches in his pocket and gets possession of the box and puts it conspicuously on the body over the dead man's heart.*) Watch her when she sees that—if you want proof !

CHRISTINE.   Open the door !   (*He forces himself to open the door and steps aside.   Christine almost falls in.   She is in a state bordering on collapse.   She throws her arms around Orin as if seeking protection from him.*)   Orin !   I got so afraid—when I found the door locked !

ORIN (*controls a furious jealous impulse to push her violently away from him—harshly*).   What made you afraid, Mother ?

CHRISTINE (*stammers*).   Why do you look at me
—like that ?   You look—so like—your father !

ORIN.   I am his son, too, remember that !

LAVINIA (*warningly*).   Orin !

CHRISTINE (*turning on Lavinia who stands by the
head of the bier*).   I suppose you've been telling him
your vile lies, you——

ORIN (*remembering his instructions, forces himself to
blurt out*).   She—she's out of her head, Mother.

CHRISTINE.   Didn't I tell you !   I knew you'd
see that !   (*Then anxiously, keeping her eyes on
Lavinia.*)   Did she tell you what she's going to do,
Orin ?   I know she's plotting something—crazy !
Did she threaten to go to the police ?   They might
not believe she's crazy——   (*Pleading desperately,
her eyes still on Lavinia.*)   You won't let her do
anything dreadful like that, will you ?

ORIN (*feeling her guilt, stammers*).   No, Mother.

CHRISTINE (*her eyes, which have been avoiding the
corpse, now fasten on the dead man's face with fascinated horror*).   No—remember your father wouldn't
want—any scandal—he mustn't be worried, he said
—he needs rest and peace——   (*She addresses the
dead man directly in a strange tone of defiant scorn.*)
You seem the same to me in death, Ezra !   You
were always dead to me !   I hate the sight of death !
I hate the thought of it !   (*Her eyes shift from*

his face and she sees the box of poison. She starts back with a stifled scream and stares at it with guilty fear.)

ORIN. Mother! For God's sake, be quiet! (*The strain snaps for him and he laughs with savage irony.*) God! To think I hoped home would be an escape from death! I should never have come back to life—from my island of peace! (*Then staring at his mother strangely.*) But that's lost now! You're my lost island, aren't you, Mother?

> (*He turns and stumbles blindly from the room. Lavinia reaches out stealthily and snatches up the box. This breaks the spell for Christine whose eyes have been fixed on it hypnotically. She looks wildly at Lavinia's frozen, accusing face.*)

LAVINIA (*in a cold, grim voice*). It was Brant who got you this—medicine to make you sleep—wasn't it?

CHRISTINE (*distractedly*). No! No! No!

LAVINIA. You're telling me it was. I knew it —but I wanted to make sure.

> (*She puts the box back in the bosom of her dress —turns, rigid and square-shouldered, and walks woodenly from the room.*)

CHRISTINE (*stares after her wildly, then her eyes fasten again on the dead man's face. Suddenly she*

166

appeals to him distractedly).   Ezra !   Don't let her harm Adam !   I am the only guilty one !   Don't let Orin—— !

> (*Then, as if she read some answer in the dead man's face, she stops in terror and, her eyes still fixed on his face, backs to the door and rushes out.*)

> (*Curtain.*)

ACT FOUR

SCENE. *The stern section of a clipper ship moored alongside a wharf in East Boston, with the floor of the wharf in the foreground. The vessel lies with her bow and amidships off left and only the part aft of the mizzenmast is visible with the curve of the stern at right. The ship is unloaded and her black side rises nine or ten feet above the level of the wharf. On the poop deck above, at right, is the wheel. At left is the chart-room and the entrance to the companionway stairs leading below to the cabin. At extreme left is the mizzen-mast, the lowest yard just visible above, the boom of the spanker extending out above the deck to the right. Below the deck the portholes show a faint light from the interior of the cabin. On the wharf the end of a warehouse is at left front.*

It is a night two days after Act Two—the day following Ezra Mannon's funeral. The moon is rising above the horizon off left rear, its light accentuating the black outlines of the ship.

Borne on the wind the melancholy refrain of the capstan chanty " Shenandoah," sung by a chantyman with the crew coming in on the chorus, drifts over the water from a ship that is weighing anchor in the harbour. Half in and half out of the shadow of the warehouse, the Chantyman lies sprawled on his back, snoring in a drunken slumber. The sound of the singing seems to strike a responsive chord in his brain, for he stirs, grunts,

*and with difficulty raises himself to a sitting
position in the moonlight beyond the shadow.*

*He is a thin, wiry man of sixty-five or so, with
a tousled mop of black hair, unkempt black beard
and moustache. His weatherbeaten face is dis-
sipated, he has a weak mouth, his big round blue
eyes are bloodshot, dreamy and drunken. But
there is something romantic, a queer troubadour-
of-the-sea quality about him.*

CHANTYMAN (*listens to the singing with critical
disapproval*). A hell of a chantyman that feller
be ! Screech owls is op'ry singers compared to
him ! I'll give him a taste of how " Shenandoah "
ought t' be sung ! (*He begins to sing in a surpris-
ingly good tenor voice, a bit blurry with booze now and
sentimentally mournful to a degree, but still managing
to get full value out of the chanty.*)

" *Oh, Shenandoah, I long to hear you—
A-way, my rolling river !
Oh, Shenandoah, I can't get near you—
Way—ay, I'm bound away
Across the wide Missouri !*

" *Oh, Shenandoah, I love your daughter
A-way, my rolling river !* "

(*He stops abruptly, shaking his head—mournfully.*)
No good ! Too drunk to do myself jestice ! Pipe
down, my John ! Sleep it off ! (*He sprawls back
on his elbows—confusedly.*) Where am I ? What
the hell difference is it ? There's plenty o' fresh

air and the moon fur a glim. Don't be so damn pertic'lar ! What ye want anyways ? Featherbed an' a grand piany ? (*He sings with a maudlin zest.*)

> " *A bottle o' wine and a bottle o' beer*
> *And a bottle of Irish whisky oh !*
> *So early in the morning*
> *The sailor likes his bottle oh !* "

(*He stops and mutters.*) Who'll buy a drink fur the slickest chantyman on the Western or any other damn ocean ? Go to hell, then ! I kin buy it myself ! (*He fumbles in his pants pocket.*) I had it in this pocket—I remember I put it there pertic'lar —ten dollars in this pocket—— (*He pulls the pocket inside out—with bewildered drunken anger.*) By Christ, it's gone ! I'm plucked clean ! (*He struggles to a sitting position.*) Where was I last ? Aye, I remember ! That yaller-haired pig with the pink dress on ! Put her arm around me so lovin' ! Told me how fine I could sing ! (*He scrambles unsteadily to his feet.*) By Christ, I'll go back an' give her a seaboot in her fat tail that'll learn her—— ! (*He takes a step but lurches into the shadow and leans against the warehouse.*) Hard down ! Heavy gales around Cape Stiff ! All is sunk but honour, as the feller says, an' there's damn little o' that afloat !

> (*He stands against the warehouse, waiting for the swaying world to subside. The companionway door on the poop deck of the*

*vessel is opened and Adam Brant comes
cautiously out. He looks around him
quickly with an uneasy suspicious air.
He is dressed in a merchant captain's
blue uniform. Satisfied that there is no
one on the deck, he comes to the rail and
stares expectantly up the wharf, off left.
His attitude is tense and nervous and he
keeps one hand in his coat pocket. The
Chantyman loses his balance, lurches forward, then back against the warehouse
with a thump. Brant leaps back from
the rail, startled, jerking a revolver from
his coat pocket—then leans over the rail
again and calls threateningly.)*

BRANT. Who's there? Come out and let me
have a look at you or by God I'll shoot!

CHANTYMAN (*stares up, startled in his turn and
momentarily sobered—hastily*). Easy goes, shipmate.
Stow that pistol! I'm doin' you no harm. (*He
lurches out into the moonlight—suddenly pugnacious.*)
Not that I'm skeered o' you or your shooter! Who
the hell are you to be threatenin' the life of an
honest chantyman? Tryin' to hold me up, air ye?
I been robbed once to-night! I'll go to the police
station and tell 'em there's a robber here——

BRANT (*hastily, with a placating air*). No harm
meant. I'm skipper of this vessel and there have
been a lot of waterfront thieves around here lately.

171

I'm lacking a watchman and I've got to keep my weather eye open.

CHANTYMAN (*again momentarily sobered—touching his forehead*). Aye—aye, sir. Mind your eye. I heer'd tell robbers broke in the " Annie Lodge's " cabin two nights back. Smashed everything and stole two hundred dollars off her skipper. Murderous, too, they be ! Near beat the watchman's brains out ! (*Then drunken pugnaciousness comes over him again.*) Think I'm one o' that gang, do ye ? Come down out o' that and I'll show ye who's a thief ! I don't give a damn if ye air a skipper ! Ye could be Bully Watermann himself an' I'd not let you insult me ! I ain't signed on your old hooker ! You've got no rights over me ! I'm on dry land, by Christ, and this is a free country and——

> (*His voice has risen to a shout. Brant is alarmed that this uproar will attract someone. He puts the pistol back in his pocket hastily and peers anxiously down the wharf. Then he interrupts the Chantyman's tirade by a sharp command.*)

BRANT. Stow your damned jaw ! Or, by the Eternal, I'll come down and pound some sense in your head !

CHANTYMAN (*automatically reacts to the voice of authority—quietly*). Aye—aye, sir. (*Then inconse-*

172

quently.) You ain't needin' a chantyman fur your next vi'ge, are ye, sir?

BRANT. I'm not sailing for a month yet. If you're still out of a job then——

CHANTYMAN (*proudly*). You don't know me, that's plain! I'm the finest damn chantyman that ever put a tune to his lip! I ain't lookin' fur berths —they're lookin' fur me! Aye! Skippers are on'y too glad to git me! Many's a time I've seed a skipper an' mates sweatin' blood to beat work out of a crew but nary a lick could they git into 'em till I raised a tune—and then there'd be full sail on her afore ye knowed it!

BRANT (*impatiently*). I'm not doubting your ability. But I'd advise you to turn in and sleep it off.

CHANTYMAN (*not heeding this—sadly*). Aye, but it ain't fur long, steam is comin' in, the sea is full o' smoky tea-kettles, the old days is dyin', an' where'll you an' me be then? (*Lugubriously drunken again.*) Everything is dyin'! Abe Lincoln is dead. I used to ship on the Mannon packets an' I seed in the paper where Ezra Mannon was dead! (*Brant starts guiltily. The Chantyman goes on maudlinly.*) Heart failure killed him, it said, but I know better! I've sailed on Mannon hookers an' been worked t' death and gotten swill fur grub, an' I know he didn't have no heart in him! Open him up an' you'd find a dried turnip! The old skinflint must have left a pile o' money. Who gits it, I wonder? Leave a widder, did he?

BRANT (*harshly*). How would I know? (*Changing the subject calculatingly.*) What are you doing here, Chantyman? I'd expect a man with your voice would be in a saloon, singing and making merry!

CHANTYMAN. So I would! So I would! But I was robbed, sir—aye—an' I know who done it —a yaller-haired wench had her arm around me. Steer clear o' gals or they'll skin your hide off an' use it fur a carpet! I warn ye, skipper! They're not fur sailormen like you an' me, 'less we're lookin' fur sorrow! (*Then insinuatingly.*) I ain't got the price of a drink, that's why I'm here, sir.

BRANT (*reaches in his pocket and tosses him down a silver coin*). Here!

CHANTYMAN (*fumbles around and finds the dollar*). Thank ye, sir. (*Then flatteringly.*) It's a fine ship you've got there, sir. Crack sail on her and she'll beat most of 'em—an' you're the kind to crack sail on, I kin tell by your cut.

BRANT (*pleased, glancing up at his ship's lofty rig*). Aye! I'll make her go right enough!

CHANTYMAN. All you need is a good chantyman to help ye. Here's " Hanging Johnny " fur ye! (*Brant starts at this. The Chantyman suddenly begins*

174

to sing the chanty " Hanging Johnny " with sentimental mournfulness.)

> " Oh, they call me Hanging Johnny
> *Away—ay—i—oh !*
> *They says I hangs for money*
> *Oh, hang, boys, hang ! "*

BRANT (*harshly*). Stop that damned dirge ! And get out of here ! Look lively now !

CHANTYMAN (*starting to go*). Aye—aye, sir. (*Then resentfully.*) I see ye ain't got much ear fur music. Good night.

BRANT (*with exasperated relief*). Good night. (*The Chantyman goes unsteadily off left, between the warehouse and the ship. He bursts again into his mournful dirge, his voice receding.*)

> " *They say I hanged my mother*
> *Away—ay—i—oh !*
> *They say I hanged my mother*
> *Oh, hang, boys, hang ! "*

(*Brant, standing by the rail looking after him, mutters a curse and starts pacing up and down the deck*) Damn that chanty ! It's sad as death ! I've a foreboding I'll never take this ship to sea. She doesn't want me now—a coward hiding behind a woman's skirts ! The sea hates a coward ! (*A woman's figure dressed in black, heavily veiled, moves stealthily out from the darkness between the ship and the warehouse, left. She sees the figure on the deck*)

*aoove her and shrinks back with a stifled gasp of fear.
Brant hears the noise. Immediately his revolver is in
his hand and he peers down into the shadows of the
warehouse.*) Who's there?

CHRISTINE (*with a cry of relief*). Adam!

BRANT. Christine! (*Then quickly.*) Go back
to the gangway. I'll meet you there. (*She goes
back. He hurries along the deck and disappears off
left to meet her. Their voices are heard and a moment
later they enter on the poop deck, from left. She leans
against him weakly and he supports her with his arm
around her.*) I have to bring you this way. I
bolted the door to the main deck.

CHRISTINE. I was so frightened! I wasn't
sure which ship! Some drunken man came along
singing——

BRANT. Aye. I just got rid of him. I fired
the watchman this morning so I'd be alone at night.
I was hoping you'd come soon. Did that drunk
see you?

CHRISTINE. No. I hid behind some boxes.
(*Then, frightened.*) Why have you got that pistol?

BRANT (*grimly*). I was going to give them a fight
for it—if things went wrong.

CHRISTINE. Adam!

BRANT. By God, you don't think I'll ever let
them take me alive, do you?

176

CHRISTINE. Please, please ! Don't talk of that for a moment ! Only hold me close to you ! Tell me you love me !

BRANT (*harshly*). It's no time ! I want to know what's happened ! (*Then immediately repentant he kisses her—with rough tenderness.*) Don't mind me ! My nerves are gone from waiting alone here not knowing anything but what I read in the papers —that he was dead. These last days have been hell !

CHRISTINE. If you knew what they have been for me !

BRANT. There's something gone wrong ! I can read that in your face ! What is it, Christine ?

CHRISTINE (*falteringly*). Vinnie knows—— ! She came into the room when he was dying ! He told her——

BRANT (*harshly*). God ! What is she going to do ? (*Then, without giving her time to answer his question, he suddenly looks around uneasily.*) Christine ! How did you get away ? She'd suspect you weren't going to your father's now. She followed you once before——

CHRISTINE. No. It's all right. This morning Orin said his cousins, the Bradfords, had invited him and Vinnie to visit them overnight at Blackridge and he was taking Vinnie with him because he thought a change would bring her back to her

senses.   I've made him think she's out of her head
with grief—so he wouldn't listen to her——

BRANT (*eagerly*).   And he believes that?

CHRISTINE (*weakly*).   Yes—he does—now—but
I don't know how long——

BRANT.   Ah !

CHRISTINE.   So I told him by all means to go.
It gave me the chance I wanted to come to you.
They went this morning.   They don't know I've
gone and even after they've found out they can't
prove where I went.   I can only stay a little while,
Adam—we've got to plan—so many things have
happened I couldn't foresee—I came to warn
you——

BRANT.   Ssshh !   Come below in the cabin !
We're fools to be talking out here.

> (*He guides her with his arm around her
> through the door to the companionway
> stairs and closes it quietly behind them.
> A pause in which the singing of the crew
> on the ship in the harbour comes mourn-
> fully over the water.   Then Orin and
> Lavinia come in stealthily along the deck
> from the left.   She is dressed in black as
> before.   He wears a long cloak over his
> uniform and has a slouch hat pulled
> down over his eyes.   Her manner is
> cold and grim.   Orin is holding in a*

*savage, revengeful rage.   They approach
the cabin skylight silently.   Orin bends
down by it to listen.   His face, in the
light from the skylight, becomes distorted
with jealous fury.   Lavinia puts a
restraining hand on his arm.*

The *scene fades out into darkness.   Several
minutes are supposed to elapse.   When
the light comes on again, a section of the
ship has been removed to reveal the
interior of the cabin, a small compartment,
the walls newly painted a light brown.
The skylight giving on the deck above is
in the middle of the ceiling.   Suspended
in the skylight is a ship's compass.   Beneath it is a pine table with three chairs,
one at rear, the other two at the table
ends, left and right.   On the table is a
bottle of whisky, half full, with a glass
and a pitcher of water.*

Built *against the right wall of the cabin is a
long narrow couch, like a bunk, with
leather cushions.   In the rear wall, at
right, is a door leading into the captain's
stateroom.   A big sideboard stands against
the left wall, centre.   Above it, a ship's
clock.   Farther back is a door opening
on the alleyway leading to the main deck.
The companionway stairs lead down to
this alleyway.*

There *is a lighted lamp on the sideboard and*

a ship's lantern, also lighted, at the right end of the table.

In the cabin, Brant is seated at the right of table, Christine to the rear of it. Her face looks haggard and ageing, the mouth pinched and drawn down at the corners, and her general appearance, the arrangement of her hair and clothes, has the dishevelled touch of the fugitive. She is just finishing her story of the murder and the events following it. He is listening tensely.

On the deck above, Orin and Lavinia are discovered as before, with Orin bending down by the transom, listening.)

CHRISTINE. When he was dying he pointed at me and told her I was guilty ! And afterwards she found the poison——

BRANT (*springing to his feet*). For God's sake, why didn't you——

CHRISTINE (*piteously*). I fainted before I could hide it ! And I had planned it all so carefully. But how could I foresee that she would come in just at that moment ? And how could I know he would talk to me the way he did ? He drove me crazy ! He kept talking of death ! He was torturing me ! I only wanted him to die and leave me alone !

BRANT (*his eyes lighting up with savage satisfaction*).

He knew before he died whose son I was, you said? By God, I'll bet that maddened him!

CHRISTINE (*repeats piteously*). I'd planned it so carefully—but something made things happen!

BRANT (*overcome by gloomy dejection, sinks down on his chair again*). I knew it! I've had a feeling in my bones! It serves me right, what has happened and is to happen! It wasn't that kind of revenge I had sworn on my mother's body! I should have done as I wanted—fought with Ezra Mannon as two men fight for love of a woman! (*With bitter self-contempt.*) I have my father's rotten coward blood in me, I think! Aye!

CHRISTINE. Adam! You make me feel so guilty!

BRANT (*rousing himself—shamefacedly*). I didn't mean to blame you, Christine. (*Then harshly.*) It's too late for regrets now, anyway. We've got to think what to do.

CHRISTINE. Yes! I'm so terrified of Vinnie! Oh, Adam, you must promise me to be on your guard every minute! If she convinces Orin you are my lover—— Oh, why can't we go away, Adam? Once we're out of her reach, she can't do anything.

BRANT. The " Flying Trades " won't be sailing for a month or more. We can't get cargo as soon as the owners thought.

CHRISTINE. Can't we go on another ship—as passengers—to the East—we could be married out there——

BRANT (*gloomily*). But everyone in the town would know you were gone. It would start suspicion——

CHRISTINE. No. Orin and Vinnie would lie to people. They'd have to for their own sakes. They'd say I was in New York with my father. Oh, Adam, it's the only thing we can do ! If we don't get out of Vinnie's reach right away I know something horrible will happen !

BRANT (*dejectedly*). Aye. I suppose it's the only way out for us now. The " Atlantis " is sailing on Friday for China. I'll arrange with her skipper to give us passage—and keep his mouth shut. She sails at daybreak Friday. You'd better meet me here Thursday night. (*Then with an effort.*) I'll write Clark and Dawson to-night they'll have to find another skipper for the " Flying Trades."

CHRISTINE (*noticing the hurt in his tone—miserably*). Poor Adam ! I know how it hurts you to give up your ship.

BRANT (*rousing himself guiltily—pats her hand—with gruff tenderness*). There are plenty of ships—but there is only one you, Christine !

CHRISTINE. I feel so guilty ! I've brought you nothing but misfortune !

THE HUNTED

BRANT. You've brought love—and the rest is only the price. It's worth it a million times! You're all mine now, anyway! (*He hugs her to him, staring over her head with sad blank eyes.*)

CHRISTINE (*her voice trembling*). But I'm afraid I'm not much to boast about having—now. I've grown old in the past few days. I'm ugly. But I'll make myself beautiful again—for you—— ! I'll make up to you for everything! Try not to regret your ship too much, Adam!

BRANT (*gruffly*). Let's not talk of her any more. (*Then forcing a wry smile.*) I'll give up the sea. I think it's done with me now, anyway! The sea hates a coward.

CHRISTINE (*trying hard to cheer him*). Don't talk like that! You have me, Adam! You have me! And we will be happy—once we're safe on your Blessed Islands! (*Then suddenly, with a little shudder.*) It's strange. Orin was telling me of an island——

> (*On the deck above, Orin, who has bent closer to the transom, straightens up with a threatening movement. Lavinia grips his arm, restraining him.*)

BRANT (*with a bitter, hopeless yearning*). Aye— the Blessed Isles—— Maybe we can still find happiness and forget! (*Then strangely, as if to himself.*) I can see them now—so close—and a million miles away! The warm earth in the moonlight, the trade winds rustling the coco-palms, the surf on the barrier reef singing a croon in your ears like a lullaby ! Aye ! There's peace and forgetfulness for us there—if we can ever find those islands now !

CHRISTINE (*desperately*). We will find them ! We will ! (*She kisses him. A pause. Suddenly she glances, in fear, at the clock.*) Look at the time ! I've got to go, Adam !

BRANT. For the love of God, watch out for Vinnie. If anything happened to you now—— !

CHRISTINE. Nothing will happen to me. But you must be on your guard in case Orin—— Good-bye, my lover ! I must go ! I must ! (*She tears herself from his arms but immediately throws herself in them again—terrified.*) Oh ! I feel so strange—so sad—as if I'd never see you again ! (*She begins to sob hysterically.*) Oh, Adam, tell me you don't regret ! Tell me we're going to be happy ! I can't bear this horrible feeling of despair !

BRANT. Of course we'll be happy ! Come now ! It's only a couple of days. (*They start for the door.*) We'll go by the main deck. It's shorter. I'll walk to the end of the wharf with you. I won't go farther. We might be seen.

CHRISTINE. Then we don't have to say good-bye for a few minutes yet ! Oh, thank God !

(They go out to the alleyway, Brant closing the door behind him. A pause. On the deck above Orin pulls a revolver from under his cloak and makes a move, as if to rush off left down to the main deck after them. Lavinia has been dreading this and throws herself in his way, grasping his arm.)

ORIN (*in a furious whisper*). Let me go!

LAVINIA (*struggling with him*). No! Be quiet! Ssshh! I hear them on the main deck! Quick! Come to his cabin!

(She urges him to the companionway door, gets him inside and shuts the door behind them. A moment later the door on the left of the cabin below is opened and they enter.)

LAVINIA. He's going to the end of the wharf. That gives us a few minutes. (*Grimly.*) You wanted proof! Well, are you satisfied now?

ORIN. Yes! God damn him! Death is too good for him! He ought to be——

LAVINIA (*sharply commanding*). Orin! Remember you promised not to lose your head. You've got to do everything exactly as we planned it, so there'll be no suspicion about us. There would be no justice if we let ourselves——

ORIN (*impatiently*). You've said all that before! Do you think I'm a fool? I'm not anxious to be hanged—for that skunk! (*Then with bitter anguish.*) I heard her asking him to kiss her! I heard her warn him against me! (*He gives a horrible chuckle.*) And my island I told her about— which was she and I—she wants to go there—with him! (*Then furiously.*) Damn you! Why did you stop me? I'd have shot his guts out in front of her!

LAVINIA (*scornfully*). Outside on deck where the shot would be sure to be heard? We'd have been arrested—and then I'd have to tell the truth to save us. She'd be hanged, and even if we managed to get off, our lives would be ruined! The only person to come off lucky would be Brant! He could die happy, knowing he'd revenged himself on us more than he ever dared hope! Is that what you want?

ORIN (*sullenly*). No.

LAVINIA. Then don't act like a fool again. (*Looks around the cabin calculatingly—then in a tone of command.*) Go and hide outside. He won't see you when he passes along the alleyway in the dark. He'll come straight in here. That's the time for you——

ORIN (*grimly*). You needn't tell me what to do. I've had a thorough training at this game—thanks to you and Father.

LAVINIA. Quick ! Go out now ! He won't be long !

ORIN (*goes to the door—then quickly*). I hear him coming.

> (*He slips out silently. She hurriedly hides herself by the sideboard at left front. A moment later Brant appears in the doorway and stands just inside it blinking in the light. He looks around the cabin sadly.*)

BRANT (*huskily*). So it's good-bye to you, " Flying Trades " ! And you're right ! I wasn't man enough for you !

> (*Orin steps through the door and with the pistol almost against Brant's body fires twice. Brant pitches forward to the floor by the table, rolls over, twitches a moment on his back and lies still. Orin springs forward and stands over the body, his pistol aimed down at it, ready to fire again.*)

LAVINIA (*stares, fascinated, at Brant's still face*). Is he—dead ?

ORIN. Yes.

LAVINIA (*sharply*). Don't stand there ! Where's the chisel you brought ? Smash open everything in his stateroom. We must make it look as if thieves killed him, remember ! Take anything valuable ! We can sink it overboard afterwards ! Hurry !

> (*Orin puts his revolver on the table and takes a chisel that is stuck in his belt under his cloak and goes into the stateroom. A moment later there is the sound of splintering wood as he prizes open a drawer.*)

LAVINIA (*goes slowly to the body and stands looking down into Brant's face. Her own is frozen and expressionless. A pause. Orin can be heard in the stateroom prizing open Brant's desk and scattering the contents of drawers around. Finally Lavinia speaks to the corpse in a grim bitter tone*). How could you love that vile old woman so ? (*She throws off this thought—harshly.*) But you're dead ! It's ended ! (*She turns away from him resolutely—then suddenly turns back and stands stiffly upright and grim beside the body and prays coldly, as if carrying out a duty.*) May God find forgiveness for your sins ! May the soul of our cousin, Adam Mannon, rest in peace ! (*Orin comes in from the stateroom and overhears the last of her prayer.*)

ORIN (*harshly*). Rest in hell, you mean ! (*He comes to her.*) I've prized open everything I could find.

LAVINIA. Then come along. Quick. There's your pistol. Don't forget that. (*She goes to the door.*)

ORIN (*putting it in his pocket*). We've got to go through his pockets to make everything look like a burglary. (*He quickly turns Brant's pockets inside out and puts the revolver he finds, along with bills and coins, watch and chain, knife, etc., into his own.*) I'll drop these overboard from the deck, along with what was in his stateroom.

> (*Having finished this, he still remains stooping over the body and stares into Brant's face, a queer fascinated expression in his own eyes.*)

LAVINIA (*uneasily*). Orin !

ORIN. By God, he does look like Father !

LAVINIA. No ! Come along !

ORIN (*as if talking to himself*). This is like my dream. I've killed him before—over and over.

LAVINIA. Orin !

ORIN. Do you remember me telling you how the faces of the men I killed came back and changed to Father's face and finally became my own ? (*He smiles grimly.*) He looks like me, too ! Maybe I've committed suicide !

LAVINIA (*frightened—gripping his arm*). Hurrv ! Someone may come !

ORIN (*not heeding her, still staring at Brant—strangely*). If I had been he I would have done what he did ! I would have loved her as he loved her—and killed Father, too—for her sake !

LAVINIA (*tensely—shaking him by the arm*). Orin, for God's sake, will you stop talking crazy and come along ? Do you want us to be found here ? (*She pulls him away forcibly.*)

ORIN (*with a last look at the dead man*). It's queer ! It's a rotten dirty joke on someone ! (*He lets her hurry him out to the alleyway.*)

(*Curtain.*)

ACT FIVE

SCENE. *The same as Act Three of " Homecoming "—*
exterior of the Mannon house. It is the following
night. The moon has just risen. The right
half of the house is in the black shadow cast by
the pine trees but the moonlight falls full on the
part to the left of the doorway. The door at
centre is open and there is a light in the hall
behind. All the shutters of the windows are
closed.

Christine is discovered walking back and forth
on the drive before the portico, passing from
moonlight into the shadow of the pines and back
again. She is in a frightful state of tension,
unable to keep still.

She sees someone she is evidently expecting
approaching the house from up the drive, off
left, and she hurries down as far as the bench
to meet her.

HAZEL (*enters from left—with a kindly smile*).
Here I am ! Seth brought your note and I
hurried over at once.

CHRISTINE (*kissing her—with unnatural effusive-*
ness). I'm so glad you've come ! I know I
shouldn't have bothered you.

HAZEL. It's no bother at all, Mrs. Mannon.
I'm only too happy to keep you company.

CHRISTINE. I was feeling so terribly sad—and

nervous here. I had let Hannah and Annie have the night off. I'm all alone. (*She sits on the bench.*) Let's sit out here. I can't bear it in the house. (*Hazel sits beside her.*)

HAZEL (*pityingly*). I know. It must be terribly lonely for you. You must miss him so much.

CHRISTINE (*with a shudder*). Please don't talk about—— He is buried ! He is gone !

HAZEL (*gently*). He is at peace, Mrs. Mannon.

CHRISTINE (*with bitter mockery*). I was like you once ! I believed in heaven ! Now I know there is only hell !

HAZEL. Ssshh ! You mustn't say that.

CHRISTINE (*rousing herself—forcing a smile*). I'm not fit company for a young girl, I'm afraid. You should have youth and beauty and freedom around you. I'm old and ugly and haunted by death ! (*Then, as if to herself—in a low desperate tone.*) I can't let myself get ugly ! I can't !

HAZEL. You're only terribly worn out. You ought to try and sleep.

CHRISTINE. I don't believe there's such a thing on this earth as sleep ! It's only in the earth one sleeps ! One must feel so at peace—at last—with all one's fears ended ! (*Then forcing a laugh.*) Good heavens, what a bore it must be for you, listening to my gloomy thoughts ! I honestly didn't send for you to——— I wanted to ask if you or Peter had heard anything from Orin and Vinnie.

HAZEL (*surprised*). Why, no. We haven't seen them since the funeral.

CHRISTINE (*forcing a smile*). They seem to have deserted me. (*Then quickly.*) I mean they should have been home before this. I can't imagine what's keeping them. They went to Blackridge to stay overnight at the Bradfords'.

HAZEL. Then there's nothing to worry about. But I don't see how they could leave you alone—just now.

CHRISTINE. Oh, that part is all right. I urged them to go. They left soon after the funeral, and afterwards I thought it would be a good opportunity for me to go to New York and see my father. He's ill, you know, but I found him so much better I decided to come home again last night. I expected Vinnie and Orin back this noon, but here it's night and no sign of them. I—I must confess I'm worried—and frightened. You can't know the horror of being all night—alone in that house ! (*She glances at the house behind her with a shudder.*)

HAZEL. Would it help you if I stayed with you to-night—I mean if they don't come ?

CHRISTINE (*eagerly*). Oh, would you ? (*Hysteri-*

cal tears come to her eyes. She kisses Hazel with impulsive gratitude.) I can't tell you how grateful I'd be ! You're so good ! (*Then forcing a laugh.*) But it's an imposition to ask you to face such an ordeal. I can't stay still. I'm terrified at every sound. You would have to sit up.

HAZEL. Losing a little sleep won't hurt me.

CHRISTINE. I mustn't sleep ! If you see me falling asleep you must promise to wake me !

HAZEL. But it's just what you need.

CHRISTINE. Yes—afterwards—but not now. I must keep awake. (*In tense desperation.*) I wish Orin and Vinnie would come !

HAZEL (*worriedly*). Perhaps Orin got worse and he wasn't able to. Oh, I hope that isn't it ! (*Then getting up.*) If I'm going to stay all night I'll have to run home and tell Mother, so she won't worry.

CHRISTINE. Yes—do. (*Then, frightened.*) You won't be long, will you ? I'm afraid—to be alone.

HAZEL (*kisses her—pityingly*). I'll be as quick as I possibly can.

> (*She walks down the drive, off left, waving her hand as she disappears. Christine stands by the bench—then begins to pace back and forth again.*)

CHRISTINE (*her eyes caught by something down the drive—in a tense whisper*). She's met someone by the gate ! Oh, why am I so afraid ! (*She turns, seized by panic, and runs to the house—then stops at the top of the steps and faces around, leaning against a column for support.*) Oh, God, I'm afraid to know !

> (*A moment later Orin and Lavinia come up the drive from the left. Lavinia is stiffly square-shouldered, her eyes hard, her mouth grim and set. Orin is in a state of morbid excitement. He carries a newspaper in his hand.*)

ORIN (*speaking to Vinnie as they enter—harshly*). You let me do the talking ! I want to be the one—— (*He sees his mother, and is startled.*) Mother! (*Then with vindictive mockery.*) Ah ! So this time at least you are waiting to meet me when I come home !

CHRISTINE (*stammers*). Orin ! What kept you—— ?

ORIN. We just met Hazel. She said you were terribly frightened at being alone here. That is strange—when you have the memory of Father for company !

CHRISTINE. You—you stayed all this time—at the Bradfords' ?

ORIN. We didn't go to the Bradfords' !

CHRISTINE (*stupidly*). You didn't go—to Blackridge ?

ORIN. We took the train there but we decided to stay right on and go to Boston instead.

CHRISTINE (*terrified*). To—Boston——?

ORIN. And in Boston we waited until the evening train got in. We met that train.

CHRISTINE. Ah !

ORIN. We had an idea you would take advantage of our being in Blackridge to be on it—and you were ! And we followed you when you called on your lover in his cabin !

CHRISTINE (*with a piteous effort at indignation*). Orin ! How dare you talk——! (*Then brokenly.*) Orin ! Don't look at me like that ! Tell me——

ORIN. Your lover ! Don't lie ! You've lied enough, Mother ! I was on deck, listening ! What would you have done if you had discovered me ? Would you have got your lover to murder me, Mother ? I heard you warning him against me ! But your warning was no use !

CHRISTINE (*chokingly*). What——? Tell me—— !

ORIN. I killed him !

CHRISTINE (*with a cry of terror*). Oh—oh ! I knew ! (*Then clutching at Orin.*) No—Orin ! You—you're just telling me that—to punish me, aren't you ? You said you loved me—you'd protect me—protect your mother—you couldn't murder—— ?

ORIN (*harshly, pushing her away*). You could murder Father, couldn't you ? (*He thrusts the newspaper into her hands, pointing to the story.*) Here ! Read that, if you don't believe me ! We got it in Boston to see whom the police would suspect. It's only a few lines. Brant wasn't important—except to you !

> (*She looks at the paper with fascinated horror. Then she lets it slip through her fingers, sinks down on the lowest step and begins to moan to herself, wringing her hands together in stricken anguish. Orin turns from her and starts to pace up and down by the steps. Lavinia stands at the left of the steps, rigid and erect, her face mask-like.*)

ORIN (*harshly*). They think exactly what we planned they should think—that he was killed by waterfront thieves. There's nothing to connect us with his death ! (*He stops by her. She stares before her, wringing her hands and moaning. He blurts out.*) Mother ! Don't moan like that ! (*She gives no sign of having heard him. He starts to pace up and down again—with savage resentment.*) Why do you grieve for that servant's bastard ? I know he was the one who planned Father's murder ! You couldn't have done that ! He got you under his influence to revenge himself ! He hypnotized you ! I saw you weren't yourself the minute I got home, remember. How else could you ever have imagined you loved that low swine ? How else could you ever have said the things—— (*He stops before her.*) I heard you planning to go with him to the island I had told you about—our island—that was you and I ! (*He starts to pace up and down again distractedly. She remains as before except that her moaning has begun to exhaust itself. Orin stops before her again and grasps her by the shoulders, kneeling on the steps beside her—desperately pleading now.*) Mother ! Don't moan like that ! You're still under his influence ! But you'll forget him ! I'll make you forget him ! I'll make you happy ! We'll leave Vinnie here and go away on a long voyage—to the South Seas——

LAVINIA (*sharply*). Orin !

ORIN (*not heeding her, stares into his mother's face. She has stopped moaning, the horror in her eyes is dying into blankness, the expression of her mouth congealing to one of numbed grief. She gives no sign of having heard him. Orin shakes her—desperately*). Mother ! Don't you hear me ? Why won't you speak to me ? Will you always love him ? Do you hate me now ? (*He sinks on his knees before her.*) Mother ! Answer me ! Say you forgive me !

LAVINIA (*with bitter scorn*). Orin ! After all that's happened, are you becoming her cry-baby again ? (*Orin starts and gets to his feet, staring at her confusedly, as if he had forgotten her existence. Lavinia speaks again in the curt, commanding tone that recalls her father.*) Leave her alone ! Go in the house ! (*As he hesitates—more sharply.*) Do you hear me ? March !

ORIN (*automatically makes a confused motion of military salute—vaguely*). Yes, sir. (*He walks mechanically up the steps—gazing up at the house—strangely.*) Why are the shutters still closed ? Father has gone. We ought to let in the moonlight.

> (*He goes into the house. Lavinia comes and stands beside her mother. Christine continues to stare blankly in front of her. Her face has become a tragic death-mask. She gives no sign of being aware of her daughter's presence. Lavinia regards her with bleak, condemning eyes.*)

LAVINIA (*finally speaks sternly*). He paid the just penalty for his crime. You know it was justice. It was the only way true justice could be done. (*Her mother starts. The words shatter her merciful numbness and awaken her to agony again. She springs to her feet and stands glaring at her daughter with a terrible look in which a savage hatred fights with horror and fear. In spite of her frozen self-*

control, Lavinia recoils before this. Keeping her eyes on her, Christine shrinks backward up the steps until she stands at the top between the two columns of the portico before the front door. Lavinia suddenly makes a motion, as if to hold her back. She calls shakenly as if the words were wrung out of her against her will.)
Mother ! What are you going to do ? You can live !

CHRISTINE (*glares at her as if this were the last insult—with strident mockery*). Live !

> (*She bursts into shrill laughter, stops it abruptly, raises her hands between her face and her daughter and pushes them out in a gesture of blotting Lavinia for ever from her sight. Then she turns and rushes into the house. Lavinia again makes a movement to follow her. But she immediately fights down this impulse and turns her back on the house determinedly, standing square-shouldered and stiff like a grim sentinel in black.*)

LAVINIA (*implacably to herself*). It is justice ! (*From the street, away off right front, Seth's thin wraith of a baritone is raised in his favourite mournful " Shenandoah," as he nears the gateway to the drive, returning from his nightly visit to the saloon.*)

> " *Oh, Shenandoah, I long to hear you*
> *A-way, my rolling river !*
> *Oh, Shenandoah, I can't get near you*

THE HUNTED

Way—ay, I'm bound away
Across the wide——"

(*There is the sharp report of a pistol from the left
ground floor of the house where Ezra Mannon's study
is. Lavinia gives a shuddering gasp, turns back to
the steps, starts to go up them, stops again and stammers
shakenly.*) It is justice! It is your justice, Father!
(*Orin's voice is heard calling from the sitting-room at
right, "What's that?" A door slams. Then Orin's
horrified cry comes from the study as he finds his mother's
body, and a moment later he rushes out frantically to
Lavinia.*)

ORIN. Vinnie! (*He seizes her arm and stammers
distractedly.*) Mother — shot herself — Father's
pistol—get a doctor—— (*Then with hopeless
anguish.*) No—it's too late—she's dead! (*Then
wildly.*) Why—why did she, Vinnie? (*With tortured self-accusation.*) I drove her to it! I wanted
to torture her! She couldn't forgive me! Why
did I have to boast about killing him? Why—— ?

LAVINIA (*frightened, puts her hand over his mouth*).
Be quiet!

ORIN (*tears her hand away—violently*). Why
didn't I let her believe burglars killed him? She
wouldn't have hated me then! She would have
forgotten him! She would have turned to me!
(*In a final frenzy of self-denunciation.*) I murdered
her!

LAVINIA (*grasping him by the shoulders*). For God's sake, will you be quiet?

ORIN (*frantically—trying to break away from her*). Let me go! I've got to find her! I've got to make her forgive me! I—— ! (*He suddenly breaks down and weeps in hysterical anguish. Lavinia puts her arm around him soothingly. He sobs despairingly.*) But she's dead—— She's gone—how can I ever get her to forgive me now?

LAVINIA (*soothingly*). Ssshh! Ssshh! You have me, haven't you? I love you. I'll help you to forget.

> (*He turns to go back into the house, still sobbing helplessly. Seth's voice comes from the drive, right, close at hand:*
>
> "*She's far across the stormy water*
> *Way-ay, I'm bound away——*"
>
> *He enters right front. Lavinia turns to face him.*)

SETH (*approaching*). Say, Vinnie, did you hear a shot—— ?

LAVINIA (*sharply*). I want you to go for Doctor Blake. Tell him Mother has killed herself in a fit of insane grief over Father's death. (*Then as he stares, dumbfounded and wondering, but keeping his face expressionless—more sharply.*) Will you remember to tell him that?

SETH (*slowly*). Ayeh. I'll tell him, Vinnie—anything you say.

> (*His face set grimly, he goes off, right front. Lavinia turns and, stiffly erect, her face stern and mask-like, follows Orin into the house.*)
>
> (*Curtain.*)

The Haunted

A Play in Four Acts
Part Three of the Trilogy

Mourning Becomes Electra

Characters

LAVINIA MANNON
ORIN, *her brother.*
PETER NILES
HAZEL, *his sister.*
SETH
AMOS AMES
IRA MACKEL
JOE SILVA
ABNER SMALL

Scenes

ACT ONE

SCENE ONE : Exterior of the Mannon house—an evening in the summer of 1866.

SCENE TWO : Sitting-room in the house (immediately follows Scene One).

ACT TWO

The study—an evening a month later.

ACT THREE

The sitting-room (immediately follows Act Two).

ACT FOUR

Same as Act One, Scene One—Exterior of the Mannon house—a late afternoon three days later.

ACT ONE

Exterior of the Mannon house (as in the two preceding plays) on an evening of a clear day in summer a year later. It is shortly after sunset but the afterglow in the sky still bathes the white temple portico in a crimson light. The columns cast black bars of shadow on the wall behind them. All the shutters are closed and the front door is boarded up, showing that the house is unoccupied.

A group of five men is standing on the drive by the bench at left, front. Seth Beckwith is there and Amos Ames, who appeared in the first Act of "Homecoming." The others are Abner Small, Joe Silva and Ira Mackel.

These four—Ames, Small, Silva and Mackel—are, as were the townsfolk of the first acts of "Homecoming" and "The Hunted," a chorus of types representing the town as a human background for the drama of the Mannons.

Small is a wiry little old man of sixty-five, a clerk in a hardware store. He has white hair and a wispy goat's beard, bright inquisitive eyes, ruddy complexion, and a shrill rasping voice. Silva is a Portuguese fishing captain—a fat, boisterous man, with a hoarse bass voice. He has matted grey hair and a big grizzled moustache. He is sixty. Mackel, who is a farmer, hobbles along with the aid of a cane. His shiny wrinkled

209

*face is oblong with square-cut white chin whiskers.
He is bald. His yellowish brown eyes are sly.
He talks in a drawling wheezy cackle.*

*All five are drunk. Seth has a stone jug in
his hand. There is a grotesque atmosphere about
these old men as of boys out on a forbidden lark.*

SMALL. God A'mighty, Seth, be you glued to
that jug ?

MACKEL. Gol durn him, he's gittin' stingy in
his old age !

SILVA (*bursts into song*).

" *A bottle of beer and a bottle of gin
And a bottle of Irish whisky oh !
So early in the morning
A sailor likes his bottle oh !* "

AMES (*derisively*). You like your bottle 'ceptin'
when your old woman's got her eye on ye !

SILVA. She's visitin' her folks to New Bedford.
What the hell I care ! (*Bursts into song again.*)

" *Hurrah ! Hurrah ! I sing the jubilee
Hurrah ! Hurrah ! Her folks has set me free !* "

AMES (*slapping him on the back*). God damn you,
Joe, you're gittin' to be a poet ! (*They all laugh.*)

SMALL. God A'mighty, Seth, ain't ye got no
heart in ye ? Watch me perishin' fur lack o'
whisky and ye keep froze to that jug ! (*He
reaches out for it.*)

THE HAUNTED

SETH. No, ye don't ! I'm on to your game ! (*With a wink at the others.*) He's aimin' to git so full of Injun courage he wouldn't mind if a ghost sot on his lap ! Purty slick you be, Abner ! Swill my licker so's you kin skin me out o' my bet !

MACKEL. That's it, Seth ! Don't let him play no skin games !

JOE. By God, if ghosts look like the livin', I'd let Ezra's woman's ghost set on my lap ! M'm ! (*He smacks his lips lasciviously.*)

AMES. Me, too ! She was a beauty !

SMALL (*with an uneasy glance at the house*). It's her ghost folks is sayin' haunts the place, ain't it ?

SETH (*with a wink at the others*). Oh, hers and a hull passel of others. The graveyard's full of Mannons and they all spend their nights at home here. You needn't worry but you'll have plenty o' company, Abner ! (*The others laugh, their mirth a bit forced, but Small looks rather sick.*)

SMALL. It ain't in our bet for you to put sech notions in my head afore I go in, be it ? (*Then forcing a perky bravado.*) Think you kin scare me ? There ain't no sech thing as ghosts !

SETH. An' I'm sayin' you're scared to prove there ain't ! Let's git our bet set out plain afore witnesses. I'm lettin' you in the Mannon house and I'm bettin' you ten dollars and a gallon of

licker you dasn't stay there till moonrise at ten
o'clock. If you come out afore then, you lose.
An' you're to stay in the dark and not even strike
a match ! Is that agreed ?

SMALL (*trying to put a brave face on it*). That's
agreed—an' it's like stealin' ten dollars off you !

SETH. We'll see ! (*Then with a grin.*) An'
you're supposed to go in sober ! But I won't
make it too dead sober ! I ain't that hard-hearted.
I wouldn't face what you'll face with a gallon under
my belt ! (*Handing him the jug.*) Here ! Take
a good swig ! You're lookin' a bit pale about
the gills a'ready !

SMALL. No sech thing ! (*But he puts the jug
to his lips and takes an enormous gulp.*)

MACKEL. Whoa thar ! Ye ain't drinkin' fur
all on us !

> (*Small hands the jug to him and he drinks
> and passes it round until it finally
> reaches Seth again. In the meantime
> Small talks to Seth.*)

SMALL. Be it all right fur me to go in afore
dark ? I'd like to know where I'm while I kin
see.

SETH. Wal, I calc'late you kin. Don't want
you runnin' into furniture an' breakin' things when
them ghosts git chasin' you ! Vinnie an' Orin's
liable to be back from Chiny afore long an' she'd

give me hell if anythin' was broke. (*The jug reaches him. He takes a drink—then sets it down on the drive.*) Come along ! I've took the screws out o' that door. I kin let you right in. (*He goes towards the portico, Small following him, whistling with elaborate nonchalance.*)

SMALL (*to the others who remain where they are*). So long, fellers. We'll have a good spree on that ten dollars.

MACKEL (*with a malicious cackle*). Mebbe ! Would you like me fur one o' your pallbearers, Abner ?

AMES. I'll comfort your old woman—providin' she'll want comfortin', which ain't likely !

SILVA. And I'll water your grave every Sunday after church ! That's the kind of man I be, by God. I don't forget my friends when they're gone !

SETH (*from the portico*). We'll all jine in, Joe ! If he ain't dead, by God, we'll drown him !

> (*They all roar with laughter. Small looks bitter. The jest strikes him as being unfeeling—All glow has faded from the sky and it is getting dark.*)

SMALL. To hell with ye ! (*Seth prizes off the board door and unlocks the inner door.*)

SETH. Come on. I'll show you the handiest

place to say your prayers. (*They go in. The group outside becomes serious.*)

AMES (*voicing the opinion of all of them*). Wal, all the same, I wouldn't be in Abner's boots. It don't do to monkey with them thin's.

MACKEL. You believe in ghosts, Amos ?

AMES. Mebbe. Who knows there ain't ?

MACKEL. Wal, I believe in 'em. Take the Nims' place out my way. Asa Nims killed his wife with a hatchet—she'd nagged him—then hung himself in the attic. I knew Ben Willett that bought the place. He couldn't live thar—had to move away. It's fallen to ruins now. Ben used to hear things clawin' at the walls an' winders and see the chairs move about. He wasn't a liar nor chicken-hearted neither.

SILVA. There is ghosts, by God ! My cousin, Manuel, he seen one ! Off on a whaler in the Injun Ocean, that was. A man got knifed and pushed overboard. After that, on moonlight nights, they'd see him a-settin' on the yards and hear him moanin' to himself. Yes, sir, my cousin Manuel, he ain't no liar neither—'ceptin' when he's drunk —and he seen him with his own eyes !

AMES (*with an uneasy glance around, reaching for the jug*). Wal, let's have a drink. (*He takes a swig just as Seth comes out of the house, shutting the door behind him.*)

MACKEL. That's Seth. He ain't anxious to stay in thar long, I notice ! (*Seth hurries down to them, trying to appear to saunter.*)

SETH (*with a forced note to his joking*). God A'mighty, ye'd ought to see Abner ! He's shyin' at the furniture covers an' his teeth are clickin' a'ready. He'll come runnin' out hell fur leather afore long. All I'm wonderin' is, has he got ten dollars.

MACKEL (*slyly*). You seem a bit shaky.

SETH (*with a scowl*). You're a liar. What're ye all lookin' glum as owls about ?

MACKEL. Been talkin' of ghosts. Do you really believe that there house is haunted, Seth, or are ye only jokin' Abner ?

SETH (*sharply*). Don't be a durned fool ! I'm on'y jokin' him, of course !

MACKEL (*insistently*). Still, it'd be only natural if it was haunted. She shot herself there. Do you think she done it fur grief over Ezra's death, like the daughter let on to folks ?

SETH. 'Course she did !

MACKEL. Ezra dyin' sudden his first night at home—that was durned queer !

SETH (*angrily*). It's durned queer old fools like you with one foot in the grave can't mind their own business in the little time left to 'em. That's what's queer !

MACKEL (*angry in his turn*). Wal, all I say is if they hadn't been Mannons with the town lickin' their boots, there'd have been queer doin's come out ! And as fur me bein' an' old fool, you're older an' a worse fool ! An' your foot's deeper in the grave than mine be !

SETH (*shaking his fist in Mackel's face*). It ain't so deep but what I kin whale the stuffin' out o' you any day in the week !

SILVA (*comes between them*). Here, you old roosters ! No fightin' allowed !

MACKEL (*subsiding grumpily*). This is a free country, ain't it ? I got a right to my opinions !

AMES (*suddenly looking off down left*). Ssshh ! Look, Seth ! There's someone comin' up the drive.

SETH (*peering*). Ayeh ! Who the hell —— ? It's Peter'n Hazel. Hide that jug, durn ye ! (*The jug is hidden under the lilacs. A moment later Hazel and Peter enter. They stop in surprise on see-ing Seth and his friends. Seth greets them self-consciously.*) Good evenin'. I was just showin' some friends around——

PETER. Hello, Seth. Just the man we're look-ing for. We've just had a telegram. Vinnie and Orin have landed in New York and——

216

(*He is interrupted by a muffled yell of terror from the house. As they all turn to look, the front door is flung open and Small comes tearing out and down the portico steps, his face chalky white and his eyes popping.*)

SMALL (*as he reaches them—terrified*). God A'mighty! I heard 'em comin' after me, and I run in the room opposite, an' I seed Ezra's ghost dressed like a judge comin' through the wall—and, by God, I run! (*He jerks a note out of his pocket and thrusts it on Seth.*) Here's your money, durn ye! I wouldn't stay in there fur a million!

(*This breaks the tension, and the old men give way to an hysterical, boisterous, drunken mirth, roaring with laughter, pounding each other on the back.*)

PETER (*sharply*). What's this all about? What was he doing in there?

SETH (*controlling his laughter, and embarrassed*). Only a joke, Peter. (*Then turning on Small— scornfully.*) That was Ezra's picture hangin' on the wall, not a ghost, ye durned idjut!

SMALL (*indignantly*). I know pictures when I see 'em, an' I knowed him. This was him! Let's get out o' here. I've had enough of this durned place!

SETH. You fellers trot along. I'll jine you

later. (*They all mutter good evenings to Peter and Hazel and go off, left front. Small's excited voice can be heard receding as he begins to embroider on the horrors of his adventure. Seth turns to Peter apologetically.*) Abner Small's always braggin' how brave he is—so I bet him he dasn't stay in there———

HAZEL (*indignantly*). Seth ! What would Vinnie say if she knew you did such things ?

SETH. There ain't no harm done. I calc'late Abner didn't break nothin'. And Vinnie wouldn't mind when she knew why I done it. I was aimin' to stop the durned gossip that's been goin' round town about this house bein' haunted. You've heard it, ain't ye ?

PETER. I heard some silly talk but didn't pay any attention———

SETH. That durned idjut female I got in to clean a month after Vinnie and Orin sailed started it. Said she'd felt ghosts around. You know how them things grow. Seemed to me Abner's braggin' gave me a good chance to stop it by turnin' it all into a joke on him folks'd laugh at. An' when I git through tellin' my story of it round town tomorrow you'll find folks'll shut up and not take it serious no more.

PETER (*appreciatively*). You're right, Seth. That was a darned slick notion ! Nothing like a joke to lay a ghost !

THE HAUNTED

SETH. Ayeh. But——— (*He hesitates—then decides to say it.*) Between you 'n' me 'n' the lamp-post, it ain't all sech a joke as it sounds—that about the hauntin', I mean.

PETER (*incredulously*). You aren't going to tell me you think the house is haunted too !

SETH (*grimly*). Mebbe, and mebbe not. All I know is I wouldn't stay in there all night if you was to give me the town !

HAZEL (*impressed but forcing a teasing tone*). Seth ! I'm ashamed of you !

PETER. First time I ever heard you say you were afraid of anything !

SETH. There's times when a man's a darn fool not to be scared ! Oh, don't git it in your heads I take stock in spirits trespassin' round in windin' sheets or no sech lunatic doin's. But there is sech a thing as evil spirit. An' I've felt it, goin' in there daytimes to see to things—like somethin' rottin' in the walls !

PETER. Bosh !

SETH (*quietly*). 'Taint bosh, Peter. There's been evil in that house since it was first built in hate—and it's kept growin' there ever since, as what's happened there has proved. You under-stand I ain't sayin' this to no one but you two. An' I'm only tellin' you fur one reason—because you're closer to Vinnie and Orin than anyone and you'd ought to persuade them, now they're back, not to live in it. (*He adds impressively.*) Fur their own good ! (*Then with a change of tone.*) An' now I've got that off my chest, tell me about 'em. When are they comin' ?

PETER. To-morrow. Vinnie asked us to open the house. So let's start right in.

SETH (*with evident reluctance*). You want to do it to-night ?

HAZEL. We must, Seth. We've got so little time. We can at least tidy up the rooms a little and get the furniture covers off.

SETH. Wal, I'll go to the barn and git lanterns. There's candles in the house. (*He turns abruptly and goes off left between the lilacs and the house.*)

HAZEL (*looking after him—uneasily*). I can't get over Seth acting so strangely.

PETER. Don't mind him. It's rum and old age.

HAZEL (*shaking her head—slowly*). No. There is something queer about this house. I've always felt it, even before the General's death and her suicide. (*She shudders.*) I can still see her sitting on that bench as she was that last night. She was so frightened of being alone. But I thought when Vinnie and Orin came back she would be all right. (*Then sadly.*) Poor Orin ! I'll never forget to my dying day the way he looked when we saw him at the funeral. I hardly recognized him, did you ?

PETER. No. He certainly was broken up.

HAZEL. And the way he acted—like someone in a trance ! I don't believe when Vinnie rushed him off on this trip to the East he knew what he was doing or where he was going or anything.

PETER. A long voyage like that was the best thing to help them both forget.

HAZEL (*without conviction*). Yes. I suppose it was—but—— (*She stops and sighs—then worriedly.*) I wonder how Orin is. Vinnie's letters haven't said much about him, or herself, for that matter— only about the trip. (*She sees Seth approaching, whistling loudly, from left, rear, with two lighted lanterns.*) Here's Seth. (*She walks up the steps to the portico. Peter follows her. She hesitates and stands looking at the house—in a low tone, almost of dread.*) Seth was right. You feel something cold grip you the moment you set foot——

PETER. Oh, nonsense ! He's got you going, too ! (*Then with a chuckle.*) Listen to him whistling to keep his courage up ! (*Seth comes in from the left. He hands one of the lanterns to Peter.*)

SETH. Here you be, Peter.

HAZEL. Well, let's go in. You better come out to the kitchen and help me first, Peter. We ought to start a fire.

(*They go in. There is a pause in which Peter can be heard opening windows behind the shutters in the downstairs rooms. Then silence. Then Lavinia enters, coming up the drive from left, front, and stands regarding the house. One is at once aware of an extraordinary change in her. Her body, formerly so thin and undeveloped, has filled out. Her movements have lost their square-shouldered stiffness. She now bears a striking resemblance to her mother in every respect, even to being dressed in the green her mother had affected. She walks to the clump of lilacs and stands there staring at the house.*)

LAVINIA (*turns back and calls coaxingly in the tone one would use to a child*).   Don't stop there, Orin ! What are you afraid of ?   Come on !

(*He comes slowly and hesitatingly in from left, front. He carries himself woodenly erect now like a soldier. His movements and attitudes have the statue-like quality that was so marked in his father. He now wears a close-cropped beard in addition to his moustache, and this accentuates his resemblance to the Judge. The Mannon semblance of his face in repose to a mask is more pronounced than ever. He has grown dreadfully thin and his black suit hangs loosely about him. His haggard*) *swarthy face is set in a blank lifeless expression.*)

LAVINIA (*glances at him uneasily—concealing her apprehension under a coaxing motherly tone*). You must be brave ! This is the test ! You have got to face it ! (*Then anxiously as he makes no reply.*) Do you feel you can—now we're here ?

ORIN (*dully*). I'll be all right—with you.

LAVINIA (*takes his hand and pats it encouragingly*). That's all I wanted—to hear you say that. (*Turning to the house.*) Look, I see a light through the shutters of the sitting-room. That must be Peter and Hazel. (*Then as she sees he still keeps his eyes averted from the house.*) Why don't you look at the house ? Are you afraid ? (*Then sharply commanding.*) Orin ! I want you to look now ! Do you hear me ?

ORIN (*dully obedient*). Yes, Vinnie. (*He jerks his head around and stares at the house and draws a deep shuddering breath.*)

LAVINIA (*her eyes on his face—as if she were willing her strength into him*). Well ? You don't see any ghosts, do you ? Tell me !

ORIN (*obediently*). No.

LAVINIA. Because there are none ! Tell me you know there are none, Orin !

ORIN (*as before*). Yes.

223

LAVINIA (*searches his face uneasily—then is apparently satisfied*). Come. Let's go in. We'll find Hazel and Peter and surprise them——

> (*She takes his arm and leads him to the steps. He walks like an automaton. When they reach the spot where his mother had sat moaning, the last time he had seen her alive [Act Five of "The Hunted"], he stops with a shudder.*)

ORIN (*stammers—pointing*). It was here—she—the last time I saw her alive——

LAVINIA (*quickly, urging him on commandingly*). That is all past and finished ! The dead have forgotten us ! We've forgotten them ! Come ! (*He obeys woodenly. She gets him up the steps and they pass into the house.*)

(*Curtain.*)

Same as Act Two of " The Hunted "—The sitting-room in the Mannon house. Peter has lighted two candles on the mantel and put the lantern on the table at front. In this dim, spotty light the room is full of shadows. It has the dead appearance of a room long shut up, and the covered furniture has a ghostly look. In the flickering candlelight the eyes of the Mannon portraits stare with a grim forbiddingness.

Lavinia appears in the doorway at rear. In the lighted room, the change in her is strikingly apparent. At a first glance, one would mistake her for her mother as she appeared in the First Act of " Homecoming." She seems a mature woman, sure of her feminine attractiveness. Her brown-gold hair is arranged as her mother's had been. Her green dress is like a copy of her mother's in Act One of " Homecoming." She comes forward slowly. The movements of her body now have the feminine grace her mother's had possessed. Her eyes are caught by the eyes of the Mannons in the portraits and she approaches as if compelled in spite of herself until she stands directly under them in front of the fireplace. She suddenly addresses them in a harsh resentful voice.

LAVINIA. Why do you look at me like that? I've done my duty by you ! That's finished and forgotten ! (*She tears her eyes from theirs and, turning away, becomes aware that Orin has not followed her into the room, and is immediately frightened and uneasy and hurries toward the door, calling :*) Orin !

ORIN (*his voice comes from the dark hall*). I'm here.

LAVINIA. What are you doing out there ? Come here ! (*Orin appears in the doorway. His face wears a dazed expression and his eyes have a wild, stricken look. He hurries to her as if seeking protection. She exclaims, frightened :*) Orin ! What is it ?

ORIN (*strangely*). I've just been in the study. I was sure she'd be waiting for me in there, where —— (*Torturedly.*) But she wasn't ! She isn't anywhere. It's only they—— (*He points to the portraits.*) They're everywhere ! But she's gone for ever. She'll never forgive me now !

LAVINIA (*harshly*). Orin ! Will you be quiet !

ORIN (*unheeding—with a sudden turn to bitter resentful defiance*). Well, let her go ! What is she to me ? I'm not her son any more ! I'm Father's ! I'm a Mannon ! And they'll welcome me home !

LAVINIA (*angrily commanding*). Stop it, do you hear me !

ORIN (*shocked back to awareness by her tone— miserably confused*). I—I didn't—don't be angry, Vinnie !

LAVINIA (*soothing him now*). I'm not angry, dear —only do get hold of yourself and be brave. (*Leading him to the sofa.*) Here. Come. Let's sit down for a moment, shall we, and get used to being home? (*They sit down. She puts an arm around him reproachfully.*) Don't you know how terribly you frighten me when you act so strangely? You don't mean to hurt me, do you?

ORIN (*deeply moved*). God knows I don't, Vinnie! You're all I have in the world! (*He takes her hand and kisses it humbly.*)

LAVINIA (*soothingly*). That's a good boy. (*Then with a cheerful matter-of-fact note.*) Hazel and Peter must be out in the kitchen. Won't you be glad to see Hazel again?

ORIN (*dully now*). You've kept talking about them all the voyage home. Why? What can they have to do with us—now?

LAVINIA. A lot. What we need most is to get back to simple normal things and begin a new life. And their friendship and love will help us more than anything to forget.

ORIN (*with sudden harshness*). Forget? I thought you'd forgotten long ago—if you ever remembered, which you never seemed to! (*Then with sombre bitterness.*) Love! What right have I—or you—to love?

LAVINIA (*defiantly*). Every right!

ORIN (*grimly*). Mother felt the same about——— (*Then with a strange, searching glance at her.*) You don't know how like Mother you've become, Vinnie. I don't mean only how pretty you've grown———

LAVINIA (*with a strange shy eagerness*). Do you really think I'm as pretty now as she was, Orin?

ORIN (*as if she hadn't interrupted*). I mean the change in your soul, too. I've watched it ever since we sailed for the East. Little by little it grew like Mother's soul—as if you were stealing hers— as if her death had set you free—to become her!

LAVINIA (*uneasily*). Now don't begin talking nonsense again, please!

ORIN (*grimly*). Don't you believe in souls any more? I think you will after we've lived in this house a while! The Mannon dead will convert you. (*He turns to the portraits mockingly.*) Ask them if I'm not right!

LAVINIA (*sharply*). Orin! What's come over you? You haven't had one of these morbid spells since we left the Islands. You swore to me you had had the last of them, or I'd never have agreed to come home.

ORIN (*with a strange malicious air*). I had to get you away from the Islands. My brotherly duty! If you'd stayed there much longer——— (*He chuckles disagreeably.*)

228

LAVINIA (*with a trace of confusion*). I don't know what you're talking about. I only went there for your sake.

ORIN (*with another chuckle*). Yes—but afterwards——

LAVINIA (*sharply*). You promised you weren't going to talk any more morbid nonsense. (*He subsides meekly. She goes on reproachfully.*) Remember all I've gone through on your account. For months after we sailed you didn't know what you were doing. I had to live in constant fear of what you might say. I wouldn't live through those horrible days again for anything on earth. And remember this homecoming is what you wanted. You told me that if you could come home and face your ghosts, you knew you could rid yourself for ever of your silly feeling of guilt about the past.

ORIN (*dully*). I know, Vinnie.

LAVINIA. And I believed you, you seemed so certain of yourself. But now you've suddenly become strange again. You frighten me. So much depends on how you start, now we're home. (*Then sharply commanding.*) Listen, Orin ! I want you to start again—by facing all your ghosts here and now ! (*He turns and his eyes remain fixed on hers from now on. She asks sternly.*) Who murdered Father ?

ORIN (*falteringly*). Brant did—for revenge be-cause——

229

LAVINIA (*more sternly*).   Who murdered Father ?
Answer me !

ORIN (*with a shudder*).   Mother was under his
influence——

LAVINIA.   That's a lie !   It was he who was
under hers.   You know the truth !

ORIN.   Yes.

LAVINIA.   She was an adulteress and a murderess,
wasn't she ?

ORIN.   Yes.

LAVINIA.   If we'd done our duty under the law,
she would have been hanged, wouldn't she ?

ORIN.   Yes.

LAVINIA.   But we protected her.   She could
have lived, couldn't she ?   But she chose to kill
herself as a punishment for her crime—of her own
free will !   It was an act of justice !   You had
nothing to do with it !   You see that now, don't
you ?   (*As he hesitates, trembling violently, she seizes
his arm fiercely.*)   Tell me !

ORIN (*hardly above a whisper*).   Yes.

LAVINIA.   And your feeling of being responsible
for her death was only your morbid imagination !
You don't feel it now !   You'll never feel it again !

ORIN.   No.

LAVINIA (*gratefully—and weakly because the strength she has willed into him has left her exhausted*). There ! You see ! You can do it when you will to ! (*She kisses him. He breaks down, sobbing weakly against her breast. She soothes him.*) There ! Don't cry ! You ought to feel proud. You've proved you can laugh at your ghosts from now on. (*Then briskly, to distract his mind.*) Come now. Help me to take off these furniture covers. We might as well start making ourselves useful.

> (*She starts to work. For a moment he helps. Then he goes to one of the windows and pushes back a shutter and stands staring out. Peter comes in the door from rear. At the sight of Lavinia he stops, startled, thinks for a second it is her mother's ghost and gives an exclamation of dread. At the same moment she sees him. She stares at him with a strange eager possessiveness. She calls softly.*)

LAVINIA. Peter ! (*She goes towards him, smiling as her mother might have smiled.*) Don't you know me any more, Peter ?

PETER (*stammers*). Vinnie ! I—I thought you were—— ! I can't realize it's you ! You've grown so like your—— (*Checking himself awkwardly.*) I mean you've changed so—and we weren't looking for you until—— (*He takes her hand automatically, staring at her stupidly.*)

LAVINIA. I know. We had intended to stay in New York to-night but we decided later we'd better come right home. (*Then taking him in with a smiling appreciative possessiveness.*) Let me look at you, Peter. You haven't gone and changed, have you? No, you're the same, thank goodness! I've been thinking of you all the way home and wondering—I was so afraid you might have.

PETER (*plucking up his courage—blurts out*). You —you ought to know I'd never change—with you! (*Then, alarmed by his own boldness, he hastily looks away from her.*)

LAVINIA (*teasingly*). But you haven't said yet you're glad to see me!

PETER (*has turned back and is staring, fascinated, at her. A surge of love and desire overcomes his timidity and he bursts out*). I—you know how much I—— ! (*Then he turns away again in confusion and takes refuge in a burst of talk.*) Gosh, Vinnie, you ought to have given us more warning. We've only just started to open the place up. I was with Hazel, in the kitchen, starting a fire——

LAVINIA (*laughing softly*). Yes. You're the same old Peter! You're still afraid of me. But you mustn't be now. I know I used to be an awful old stick, but——

PETER. Who said so? You were not! (*Then with enthusiasm.*) Gosh, you look so darned pretty —and healthy. Your trip certainly did you good!

(*Staring at her again, drinking her in.*) I can't get over seeing you dressed in colour. You always used to wear black.

LAVINIA (*with a strange smile*). I was dead then.

PETER. You ought always to wear colour.

LAVINIA (*immensely pleased*). Do you think so ?

PETER. Yes. It certainly is becoming. I—— (*Then, embarrassed, he changes the subject:*) But where's Orin ?

LAVINIA (*turning to look round*). Why, he was just here. (*She sees him at the window.*) Orin, what are you doing there ? Here's Peter. (*Orin closes the shutter he has pushed open and turns back from the window. He comes forward, his eyes fixed in a strange preoccupation, as if he were unaware of their presence. Lavinia watches him uneasily and speaks sharply.*) Don't you see Peter ? Why don't you speak to him ? You mustn't be so rude.

PETER (*good-naturedly*). Give him a chance. Hello, Orin. Darned glad to see you back. (*They shake hands. Peter has difficulty in hiding his pained surprise at Orin's sickly appearance.*)

ORIN (*rousing himself, forces a smile and makes an effort at his old friendly manner with Peter*). Hello, Peter. You know I'm glad to see you without any polite palaver. Vinnie is the same old bossy fuss-buzzer—you remember—always trying to teach me manners !

PETER. You bet I remember ! But I say, hasn't she changed, though ? I didn't know her, she's grown so fat ! And I was just telling her how well she looked in colour. Don't you agree ?

ORIN (*in a sudden strange tone of jeering malice*). Did you ask her why she stole Mother's colours ? I can't see why—yet—and I don't think she knows herself. But it will prove a strange reason, I'm certain of that, when I do discover it !

LAVINIA (*making a warning sign to Peter not to take this seriously—forcing a smile*). Don't mind him, Peter.

ORIN (*his tone becoming sly, insinuating and mocking*). And she's become romantic ! Imagine that ! Influence of the " dark and deep blue ocean "— and of the Islands, eh, Vinnie ?

PETER (*surprised*). You stopped at the Islands ?

ORIN. Yes. We took advantage of our being on a Mannon ship to make the captain touch there on the way back. We stopped a month. (*With resentful bitterness.*) But they turned out to be Vinnie's islands, not mine. They only made me sick—and the naked women disgusted me. I guess I'm too much of a Mannon, after all, to turn into a pagan. But you should have seen Vinnie with the men—— !

LAVINIA (*indignantly, but with a certain guiltiness*). How can you—— !

THE HAUNTED

ORIN (*jeeringly*). Handsome and romantic-looking, weren't they, Vinnie?—with coloured rags around their middles and flowers stuck over their ears! Oh, she was a bit shocked at first by their dances, but afterwards she fell in love with the Islanders. If we'd stayed another month, I know I'd have found her some moonlight night dancing under the palm trees—as naked as the rest!

LAVINIA. Orin! Don't be disgusting!

ORIN (*points to the portraits mockingly*). Picture, if you can, the feelings of the God-fearing Mannon dead at that spectacle!

LAVINIA (*with an anxious glance at Peter*). How can you make up such disgusting fibs?

ORIN (*with a malicious chuckle*). Oh, I wasn't as blind as I pretended to be! Do you remember Avahanni?

LAVINIA (*angrily*). Stop talking like a fool! (*He subsides meekly again. She forces a smile and a motherly tone.*) You're a naughty boy, do you know it? What will Peter think? Of course, he knows you're only teasing me—but you shouldn't go on like that. It isn't nice. (*Then changing the subject abruptly.*) Why don't you go and find Hazel? Here. Let me look at you. I want you to look your best when she sees you. (*She arranges him as a mother would a boy, pulling down his coat, giving a touch to his shirt and tie. Orin straightens woodenly*

235

to a soldierly attention.   She is vexed by this.)   Don't stand like a ramrod !   You'd be so handsome if you'd only shave off that silly beard and not carry yourself like a tin soldier !

ORIN (*with a sly cunning air*).   Not look so much like Father, eh ?   More like a romantic clipper captain, is that it ?   (*As she starts and stares at him, as in fear, he smiles an ugly taunting smile.*)   Don't look so frightened, Vinnie !

LAVINIA (*with an apprehensive glance at Peter— pleading and at the same time warning*).   Ssshh ! You weren't to talk nonsense, remember !   (*Giving him a final pat.*)   There !   Now run along to Hazel.

ORIN (*looks from her to Peter suspiciously*).   You seem damned anxious to get rid of me.

> (*He turns and stalks stiffly with hurt dignity from the room.   Lavinia turns to Peter. The strain of Orin's conduct has told on her.   She seems suddenly weak and frightened.*)

PETER (*in shocked amazement*).   What's come over him ?

LAVINIA (*in a strained voice*).   It's the same thing —what the war did to him—and on top of that Father's death—and the shock of Mother's suicide.

PETER (*puts his arm around her impulsively—*

comfortingly). It'll be all right! Don't worry, Vinnie!

LAVINIA (*nestling against him gratefully*). Thank you, Peter. You're so good. (*Then looking into his eyes.*) Do you still love me, Peter?

PETER. Don't have to ask that, do you? (*He squeezes her awkwardly—then stammers.*) But do you—think now—you maybe—can love me?

LAVINIA. Yes!

PETER. You really mean that?

LAVINIA. Yes! I do! I've thought of you so much! Things were always reminding me of you—the ship and the sea—everything that was honest and clean! And the natives on the Islands reminded me of you too. They were so simple and fine—— (*Then hastily.*) You mustn't mind what Orin was saying about the Islands. He's become a regular bigoted Mannon.

PETER (*amazed*). But, Vinnie—— !

LAVINIA. Oh, I know it must sound funny hearing me talk like that. But remember I'm only half Mannon. (*She looks at the portraits defiantly.*) And I've done my duty by them! They can't say I haven't!

PETER (*mystified but happy*). Gosh, you certainly have changed! But I'm darned glad!

LAVINIA. Orin keeps teasing that I was flirting

with that native he spoke about, simply because he used to smile at me and I smiled back.

PETER (*teasingly*). Now, I'm beginning to get jealous, too.

LAVINIA. You mustn't. He made me think of you. He made me dream of marrying you—and everything.

PETER. Oh, well then, I take it all back! I owe him a vote of thanks! (*He hugs her.*)

LAVINIA (*dreamily*). I loved those Islands. They finished setting me free. There was something there mysterious and beautiful—a good spirit—of love—coming out of the land and sea. It made me forget death. There was no hereafter. There was only this world—the warm earth in the moonlight—the trade wind in the cocoa palms—the surf on the reef—the fires at night and the drum throbbing in my heart—the natives dancing naked and innocent—without knowledge of sin! (*She checks herself abruptly as if frightened.*) But what in the world! I'm running on like a regular chatterbox. You must think I've become awfully scatter-brained!

PETER (*with a chuckle*). Gosh, no! I'm glad you've grown that way! You never used to say a word unless you had to!

LAVINIA (*suddenly filled with grateful love for him, lets herself go and throws her arms around him*). Oh,

Peter, hold me close to you ! I want to feel love !
Love is all beautiful ! I never used to know that !
I was a fool ! (*She kisses him passionately. He
returns it, aroused and at the same time a little shocked
by her boldness. She goes on longingly.*) We'll be
married soon, won't we, and settle out in the
country away from folks and their evil talk ? We'll
make an island for ourselves on land, and we'll have
children and love them and teach them to love life
so that they can never be possessed by hate and
death ! (*She gives a start—in a whisper as if to
herself.*) But I'm forgetting Orin !

PETER. What's Orin got to do with us marrying ?

LAVINIA. I can't leave him—until he's well
again. I'd be afraid——

PETER. Let him live with us.

LAVINIA (*with sudden intensity*). No ! I want to
be rid of the past ! (*Then after a quick look at him
—in a confiding tone.*) I want to tell you what's
wrong with Orin—so you and Hazel can help me.
He feels guilty about Mother killing herself. You
see, he'd had a quarrel with her that last night. He
was jealous and mad and said things he was sorry
for after and it preyed on his mind until he blames
himself for her death.

PETER. But that's crazy !

LAVINIA. I know it is, Peter, but you can't do

239

anything with him when he gets his morbid spells. Oh, I don't mean he's the way he is to-night most of the time. Usually he's like himself, only quiet and sad—so sad it breaks my heart to see him— like a little boy who's been punished for something he didn't do. Please tell Hazel what I've told you, so she'll make allowances for any crazy thing he might say.

PETER. I'll warn her. And now don't you worry any more about him. We'll get him all right again one way or another.

LAVINIA (*again grateful for his simple goodness— lovingly*). Bless you, Peter !

> (*She kisses him. As she does so, Hazel and Orin appear in the doorway at rear. Hazel is a bit shocked, then smiles happily. Orin starts as if he'd been struck. He glares at them with jealous rage and clenches his fists as if he were going to attack them.*)

HAZEL (*with a teasing laugh*). I'm afraid we're interrupting, Orin. (*Peter and Vinnie jump apart in confusion.*)

ORIN (*threateningly*). So that's it ! By God —— !

LAVINIA (*frightened, but managing to be stern*). Orin !

ORIN (*pulls himself up sharply—confusedly, forcing a sickly smile*).   Don't be so solemn—Fuss Buzzer ! I was only trying to scare you—for a joke ! (*Turning to Peter and holding out his hand, his smile becoming ghastly.*)   I suppose congratulations are in order. I—I'm glad.

> (*Peter takes his hand awkwardly.   Hazel moves towards Lavinia to greet her, her face full of an uneasy bewilderment. Lavinia stares at Orin with eyes full of dread.*)

(Curtain.)

ACT TWO

SCENE. *Same as Act Three of " The Hunted "—Ezra Mannon's study—on an evening a month later. The shutters of the windows are closed. Candles on the mantel above the fireplace light up the portrait of Ezra Mannon in his judge's robes. Orin is sitting in his father's chair at left of table, writing by the light of a lamp. A small pile of manuscript is stacked by his right hand. He is intent on his work. He has aged in the intervening month. He looks almost as old now as his father in the portrait. He is dressed in black and the resemblance between the two is uncanny. A grim smile of satisfaction twitches his lips as he stops writing and reads over the paragraph he has just finished. Then he puts the sheet down and stares up at the portrait, sitting back in his chair.*

ORIN (*sardonically, addressing the portrait*). The truth, the whole truth and nothing but the truth ! Is that what you're demanding, Father ? Are you sure you want the whole truth ? What will the neighbours say if this whole truth is ever known ? (*He chuckles grimly.*) A ticklish decision for you, Your Honour ! (*There is a knock on the door. He hastily grabs the script and puts it in the drawer of the desk.*) Who's there ?

LAVINIA. It's I.

ORIN (*hastily locking the drawer and putting the key in his pocket*). What do you want?

LAVINIA (*sharply*). Please open the door!

ORIN. All right. In a minute.

> (*He hurriedly straightens up the table and grabs a book at random from the bookcase and lays it open on the table as if he had been reading. Then he unlocks the door and comes back to his chair as Lavinia enters. She wears a green velvet gown similar to that worn by Christine in Act Three of " Homecoming." It sets off her hair and eyes. She is obviously concealing beneath a surface calm a sense of dread and desperation.*)

LAVINIA (*glances at him suspiciously, but forces a casual air*). Why did you lock yourself in? (*She comes over to the table.*) What are you doing?

ORIN. Reading.

LAVINIA (*picks up the book*). Father's law books?

ORIN (*mockingly*). Why not? I'm considering studying law. He wanted me to, if you remember.

LAVINIA. Do you expect me to believe that, Orin? What is it you're really doing?

ORIN. Curious, aren't you?

LAVINIA (*forcing a smile*). Good gracious, why

wouldn't I be? You've acted so funnily lately, locking yourself in here with the blinds closed and the lamp burning even in the daytime. It isn't good for you staying in this stuffy room in this weather. You ought to get out in the fresh air.

ORIN (*harshly*). I hate the daylight. It's like an accusing eye! No, we've renounced the day, in which normal people live—or rather it has renounced us. Perpetual night—darkness of death in life—that's the fitting habitat for guilt! You believe you can escape that, but I'm not so foolish!

LAVINIA. Now you're being stupid again!

ORIN. And I find artificial light more appropriate for my work—man's light, not God's—man's feeble striving to understand himself, to exist for himself in the darkness! It's a symbol of his life —a lamp burning out in a room of waiting shadows!

LAVINIA (*sharply*). Your work? What work?

ORIN (*mockingly*). Studying the law of crime and punishment, as you saw.

LAVINIA (*forcing a smile again and turning away from him*). All right, if you won't tell me. Go on being mysterious, if you like. (*In a tense voice.*) It's so close in here! It's suffocating! It's bad for you! (*She goes to the window and throws the shutters open and looks out.*) It's black as pitch tonight. There isn't a star.

ORIN (*sombrely*). Darkness without a star to guide us ! Where are we going, Vinnie ? (*Then with a mocking chuckle.*) Oh, I know you think you know where you're going, but there's many a slip, remember !

LAVINIA (*her voice strident, as if her will were snapping*). Be quiet ! Can't you think of anything but—— (*Then controlling herself, comes to him—gently.*) I'm sorry. I'm terribly nervous to-night. It's the heat, I suppose. And you get me so worried with your incessant brooding over the past. It's the worst thing for your health. (*She pats him on the arm—soothingly.*) That's all I'm thinking about, dear.

ORIN. Thank you for your anxiety about my health ! But I'm afraid there isn't much hope for you there ! I happen to feel quite well !

LAVINIA (*whirling on him—distractedly*). How can you insinuate such horrible—— ! (*Again controlling herself with a great effort, forcing a smile.*) But you're only trying to rile me—and I'm not going to let you. I'm so glad you're feeling better. You ate a good supper to-night—for you. The long walk we took with Hazel did you good.

ORIN (*dully*). Yes. (*He slumps down in his chair at left of table.*) Why is it you never leave me alone with her more than a minute ? You approved of my asking her to marry me—and now we're engaged you never leave us alone ! (*Then with a bitter smile.*)

But I know the reason well enough. You're afraid I'll let something slip.

LAVINIA (*sits in the chair opposite him—wearily*). Can you blame me, the way you've been acting?

ORIN (*sombrely*). No. I'm afraid myself of being too long with her alone—afraid of myself. I have no right in the same world with her. And yet I feel so drawn to her purity! Her love for me makes me appear less vile to myself! (*Then with a harsh laugh.*) And, at the same time, a million times more vile, that's the hell of it! So I'm afraid you can't hope to get rid of me through Hazel. She's another lost island! It's wiser for you to keep Hazel away from me, I warn you. Because when I see love for a murderer in her eyes my guilt crowds up in my throat like poisonous vomit and I long to spit it out—and confess!

LAVINIA (*in a low voice*). Yes, that is what I live in terror of—that in one of your fits you'll say something before someone—now after it's all past and forgotten—when there isn't the slightest suspicion——

ORIN (*harshly*). Were you hoping you could escape retribution? You can't! Confess and atone to the full extent of the law! That's the only way to wash the guilt of our mother's blood from our souls!

LAVINIA (*distractedly*). Ssshh! Will you stop!

ORIN. Ask our father, the Judge, if it isn't ! He knows ! He keeps telling me !

LAVINIA. Oh, God ! Over and over and over ! Will you never lose your stupid guilty conscience ! Don't you see how you torture me ? You're becoming my guilty conscience, too ! (*With an instinctive flare-up of her old jealousy.*) How can you still love that vile woman so—when you know all she wanted was to leave you without a thought and marry that——

ORIN (*with fierce accusation*). Yes ! Exactly as you're scheming now to leave me and marry Peter ! But, by God, you won't ! You'll damn soon stop your tricks when you know what I've been writing !

LAVINIA (*tensely*). What have you written ?

ORIN (*his anger turned to gloating satisfaction*). Ah ! That frightens you, does it ? Well, you better be frightened !

LAVINIA. Tell me what you've written !

ORIN. None of your damned business.

LAVINIA. I've got to know !

ORIN. Well, as I've practically finished it—I suppose I might as well tell you. At his earnest solicitation—(*he waves a hand to the portrait mockingly*) as the last male Mannon—thank God for that, eh !—I've been writing the history of our family ! (*He adds with a glance at the portrait and a malicious chuckle*.) But I don't wish to convey that he approves of all I've set down—not by a damned sight !

LAVINIA (*trying to keep calm—tensely*).   What kind of history do you mean ?

ORIN.   A true history of all the family crimes, beginning with Grandfather Abe's—all of the crimes, including ours, do you understand ?

LAVINIA (*aghast*).   Do you mean to tell me you've actually written——

ORIN.   Yes !   I've tried to trace to its secret hiding-place in the Mannon past the evil destiny behind our lives !   I thought if I could see it clearly in the past I might be able to foretell what fate is in store for us, Vinnie—but I haven't dared predict that—not yet—although I can guess—— (*He gives a sinister chuckle.*)

LAVINIA.   Orin !

ORIN.   Most of what I've written is about you ! I found you the most interesting criminal of us all !

LAVINIA (*breaking*).   How can you say such dreadful things to me, after all I——

ORIN (*as if he hadn't heard—inexorably*).   So many strange hidden things out of the Mannon past combine in you !   For one example, do you remember the first mate, Wilkins, on the voyage to 'Frisco ?   Oh, I know you thought I was in a

stupor of grief—but I wasn't blind ! I saw how
you wanted him !

LAVINIA (*angrily, but with a trace of guilty confusion*).
I never gave him a thought ! He was an officer
of the ship to me, and nothing more !

ORIN (*mockingly*). Adam Brant was a ship's
officer, too, wasn't he ? Wilkins reminded you of
Brant——

LAVINIA. No !

ORIN. And that's why you suddenly discarded
mourning in 'Frisco and bought new clothes—in
Mother's colours !

LAVINIA (*furiously*). Stop talking about her !
You'd think, to hear you, I had no life of my own !

ORIN. You wanted Wilkins just as you'd wanted
Brant !

LAVINIA. That's a lie !

ORIN. You're doing the lying ! You know
damned well that behind all your pretence about
Mother's murder being an act of justice was your
jealous hatred ! She warned me of that and I see
it clearly now ! You wanted Brant for yourself !

LAVINIA (*fiercely*). It's a lie ! I hated him !

ORIN. Yes, after you knew he was her lover !
(*He chuckles with a sinister mockery.*) But we'll let
that pass for the present—I know it's the last thing

you could ever admit to yourself !—and come to
what I've written about your adventures on my lost
islands.   Or should I say, Adam Brant's islands !
He had been there too, if you'll remember !   Probably he'd lived with one of the native women !   He
was that kind !   Were you thinking of that when
we were there ?

LAVINIA (*chokingly*).   Stop it !   I—I warn you—
I won't bear it much longer !

ORIN (*as if he hadn't heard—in the same sinister
mocking tone*).   What a paradise the Islands were
for you, eh ?   All those handsome men staring at
you and your strange beautiful hair !   It was then
you finally became pretty—like Mother !   You
knew they all desired you, didn't you ?   It filled
you with pride !   Especially Avahanni !   You
watched him stare at your body through your
clothes, stripping you naked !   And you wanted
him !

LAVINIA.   No !

ORIN.   Don't lie !   (*He accuses her with fierce
jealousy.*)   What did you do with him the night I
was ill and you went to watch their shameless
dance ?   Something happened between you !   I saw
your face when you came back and stood with him
in front of our hut !

LAVINIA (*quietly—with simple dignity now*).   I had
kissed him good night, that was all—in gratitude !
He was innocent and good.   He had made me feel

for the first time in my life that everything about love could be sweet and natural.

ORIN. So you kissed him, did you? And that was all?

LAVINIA (*with a sudden flare of deliberately evil taunting that recalls her mother in the last act of "Homecoming," when she was goading Ezra Mannon to fury just before his murder*). And what if it wasn't? I'm not your property! I have a right to love!

ORIN (*reacting as his father had—his face grown livid—with a hoarse cry of fury grabs her by the throat*). You—you whore! I'll kill you! (*Then suddenly he breaks down and becomes weak and pitiful.*) No! You're lying about him, aren't you? For God's sake, tell me you're lying, Vinnie!

LAVINIA (*strangely shaken and trembling—stammers*). Yes—it was a lie—how could you believe I—— Oh, Orin, something made me say that to you— against my will—something rose up in me—like an evil spirit!

ORIN (*laughs wildly*). Ghosts! You never seemed so much like Mother as you did just then!

LAVINIA (*pleading distractedly*). Don't talk about it! Let's forget it ever happened! Forgive me! Please forget it!

ORIN. All right—if the ghosts will let us forget! (*He stares at her fixedly for a moment—then satisfied.*)

I believe you about Avahanni. I never really suspected, or I'd have killed him—and you too ! I hope you know that ! (*Then with his old obsessed insistence.*) But you were guilty in your mind just the same !

LAVINIA (*in a flash of distracted anger*). Stop harping on that ! Stop torturing me or I—— ! I've warned you ! I warn you again ! I can't bear any more ! I won't !

ORIN (*with a mocking diabolical sneer—quietly*). Then why don't you murder me ? I'll help you plan it, as we planned Brant's, so there will be no suspicion on you ! And I'll be grateful ! I loathe my life !

LAVINIA (*speechless with horror—can only gasp*). Oh !

ORIN (*with a quiet mad insistence*). Can't you see I'm now in Father's place and you're Mother ? That's the evil destiny out of the past I haven't dared predict ! I'm the Mannon you're chained to ! So isn't it plain——

LAVINIA (*putting her hands over her ears*). For God's sake, won't you be quiet ! (*Then suddenly her horror turning into a violent rage—unconsciously repeating the exact threat she had goaded her mother to make to her in Act Two of " Homecoming."*) Take care, Orin ! You'll be responsible if—— ! (*She stops abruptly, terrified by her own words.*)

252

ORIN (*with a diabolical mockery*).   If what ?   If I should die mysteriously of heart failure ?

LAVINIA.   Leave me alone !   Leave me alone ! Don't keep saying that !   How can you be so horrible ?   Don't you know I'm your sister, who loves you, who would give her life to bring you peace ?

ORIN (*with a change to a harsh, threatening tone*). I don't believe you !   I know you're plotting something !   But you look out !   I'll be watching you ! And I warn you I won't stand your leaving me for Peter !   I'm going to put this confession I've written in safe hands—to be read in case you try to marry him—or if I should die——

LAVINIA (*frantically grabbing his arm and shaking him fiercely*).   Stop having such thoughts !   Stop making me have them !   You're like a devil torturing me !   I won't listen !

> (*She breaks down and sobs brokenly.   Orin,
> dazed, stares at her—seems half to
> come back to his natural self and the
> wild look fades from his eyes, leaving
> them glazed and lifeless.*)

ORIN (*strangely*).   Don't cry.   The damned don't cry. (*He sinks down heavily in his father's chair and stares at the floor.   Suddenly he says harshly again :*)   Go away, will you ?   I want to be alone— to finish my work.

MOURNING BECOMES ELECTRA

(Still sobbing, her hand over her eyes, Lavinia feels blindly for the door and goes out, closing it after her. Orin unlocks the table drawer, pulls out his manuscript, and takes up his pen.)

(Curtain.)

ACT THREE

SCENE. *Same as Act One, Scene Two—the sitting-room. The lamp on the table is lighted but turned low. Two candles are burning on the mantel over the fireplace at right, shedding their flickering light on the portrait of Abe Mannon above, and of the other Mannons on the walls on each side of him. The eyes of the portraits seem to possess an intense bitter life, with their frozen stare " looking over the head of life, cutting it dead for the impropriety of living," as Orin had said of his father in Act Two of " The Hunted."*

No time has elapsed since the preceding act. Lavinia enters from the hall in the rear, having just come from the study. She comes to the table and turns up the lamp. She is in a terrific state of tension. The corners of her mouth twitch, she twines and untwines the fingers of her clasped hands with a slow wringing movement which recalls her mother in the last act of " The Hunted."

LAVINIA (*torturedly—begins to pace up and down, muttering her thoughts aloud*). I can't bear it ! Why does he keep putting his death in my head ? He would be better off if—— Why hasn't he the courage—— ? (*Then in a frenzy of remorseful anguish, her eyes unconsciously seeking the Mannon portraits on the right wall, as if they were the visible symbol of her God.*) Oh, God, don't let me have such thoughts ! You know I love Orin ! Show me the way to save him ! Don't let me think of death ! I couldn't bear another death ! Please ! Please !

> (*At a noise from the hall she controls herself and pretends to be glancing through a book on the table. Seth appears in the doorway.*)

SETH. Vinnie !

LAVINIA. What is it, Seth ?

SETH. That durned idjut, Hannah, is throwin' fits agin. Went down cellar and says she felt ha'nts crawlin' behind her. You'd better come and git her calmed down—or she'll be leavin'. (*Then he adds disgustedly :*) That's what we git fur freein' 'em !

LAVINIA (*wearily*). All right. I'll talk to her.

> (*She goes out with Seth. A pause. Then a ring from the front door bell. A moment later Seth can be seen coming back along the hall. He opens the front door and is heard greeting Hazel and Peter and follows them in as they enter the room.*)

SETH. Vinnie's just seein' to somethin'. You set down and she'll be here soon as she kin.

PETER. All right, Seth.

THE HAUNTED

(*Seth goes out again. They come forward and sit down. Peter looks hearty and good-natured, the same as ever, but Hazel's face wears a nervous, uneasy look although her air is determined.*)

PETER. I'll have to run along soon and drop in at the Council meeting. I can't get out of it. I'll be back in half an hour—maybe sooner.

HAZEL (*suddenly with a little shiver*). I hate this house now. I hate coming here. If it wasn't for Orin—— He's getting worse. Keeping him shut up here is the worst thing Vinnie could do.

PETER. He won't go out. You know very well she has to force him to walk with you.

HAZEL. And comes along herself ! Never leaves him alone, or hardly a second !

PETER (*with a grin*). Oh, that's what you've got against her, eh ?

HAZEL (*sharply*). Don't be silly, Peter ! I simply think, and I'd say it to her face, that she's a bad influence for Orin ! I feel there's something awfully wrong—somehow. He scares me at times —and Vinnie—I've watched her looking at you. She's changed so. There's something bold about her.

PETER (*getting up*). If you're going to talk like that—— ! You ought to be ashamed, Hazel !

257

HAZEL. Well, I'm not ! I've got some right to say something about how he's cared for ! And I'm going to from now on ! I'm going to make her let him visit us for a time. I've asked Mother and she'll be glad to have him.

PETER. Say, I think that's a darned good notion for both of them. She needs a rest from him, too.

HAZEL. Vinnie doesn't think it's a good notion ! I mentioned it yesterday and she gave me such a look ! (*Determinedly*.) But I'm going to make him promise to come over to-morrow, no matter what she says !

PETER (*soothingly, patting her shoulder*). Don't get angry now—about nothing. I'll help you persuade her to let him come. (*Then with a grin*.) I'll help you do anything to help Orin get well— if only for selfish reasons. As long as Vinnie's tied down to him we can't get married.

HAZEL (*stares at him—slowly*). Do you really want to marry her—now ?

PETER. Why do you ask such a fool question ? What do you mean, do I want to now ?

HAZEL (*her voice trembles and she seems about to burst into tears*). Oh, I don't know, Peter ! I don't know !

PETER (*sympathetic and at the same time exasperated*). What in the dickens is the matter with you ?

HAZEL (*hears a noise from the hall and collects herself—warningly*). Ssshh !

> (*Orin appears in the doorway at rear. He glances at them, then quickly around the room to see if Lavinia is there. They both greet him with " Hello, Orin."*)

ORIN. Hello ! (*Then in an excited whisper, coming to them.*) Where's Vinnie ?

HAZEL. She's gone to see to something, Seth said.

PETER (*glancing at his watch*). Gosh, I've got to hurry to that darned Council meeting.

ORIN (*eagerly*). You're going ?

PETER (*jokingly*). You needn't look so darned pleased about it ! It isn't polite !

ORIN. I've got to see Hazel alone !

PETER. All right ! You don't have to put me out !

> (*He grins, slapping Orin on the back and goes out. Orin follows him with his eyes until he hears the front door close behind him.*)

ORIN (*turning to Hazel—with queer furtive excitement*). Listen, Hazel ! I want you to do something ! But wait ! I've got to get—— (*He rushes out and can be heard going across the hall to the study. Hazel looks after him anxiously. A moment later he hurries back with a big sealed envelope in his hand which he gives to Hazel, talking breathlessly, with nervous jerks of his head, as he glances apprehensively at the door.)* Here! Take this! Quick! Don't let her see it! I want you to keep it in a safe place and never let anyone know you have it! It will be stolen if I keep it here! I know her! Will you promise?

HAZEL. But—what is it, Orin?

ORIN. I can't tell you. You mustn't ask me. And you must promise never to open it—unless something happens to me.

HAZEL *(frightened by his tone).* What do you mean?

ORIN. I mean if I should die—or—but this is the most important, if she tries to marry Peter— the day before the wedding—I want you to make Peter read what's inside.

HAZEL. You don't want her to marry Peter?

ORIN. No! She can't have happiness! She's got to be punished! *(Suddenly taking her hand— excitedly.)* And listen, Hazel! You mustn't love me any more. The only love I can know now is the love of guilt for guilt which breeds more guilt— until you get so deep at the bottom of hell there is no lower you can sink and you rest there in peace! *(He laughs harshly and turns away from her.)*

HAZEL. Orin ! Don't talk like that ! (*Then conquering her horror—resolutely tender and soothing.*) Ssshh ! Poor boy ! Come here to me. (*He comes to her. She puts an arm round him.*) Listen. I know something is worrying you—and I don't want to seem prying—but I've had such a strong feeling at times that it would relieve your mind if you could tell me what it is. Haven't you thought that, Orin ?

ORIN (*longingly*). Yes ! Yes ! I want to confess to your purity ! I want to be forgiven ! (*Then checking himself abruptly as he is about to speak—dully.*) No. I can't. Don't ask me. I love her.

HAZEL. But, you silly boy, Vinnie told Peter herself what it is and told him to tell me.

ORIN (*staring at her wildly*). What did she tell ?

HAZEL. About your having a quarrel with your poor mother that night before she—and how you've brooded over it until you blame yourself for her death.

ORIN (*harshly*). I see ! So in case I did tell you—oh, she's cunning ! But not cunning enough this time ! (*Vindictively.*) You remember what I've given you, Hazel, and you do exactly what I said with it. (*Then with desperate pleading.*) For God's sake, Hazel, if you love me help me to get away from here—or something terrible will happen !

HAZEL. That's just what I want to do ! You come over to-morrow and stay with us.

ORIN (*bitterly*). Do you suppose for a moment she'll ever let me go ?

HAZEL. But haven't you a right to do as you want to ?

ORIN (*furtively*). I could sneak out when she wasn't looking—and then you could hide me and when she came for me tell her I wasn't there.

HAZEL (*indignantly*). I won't do any such thing ! I don't tell lies, Orin ! (*Then scornfully.*) How can you be so scared of Vinnie ?

ORIN (*hearing a noise from the hall—hastily*). Ssshh ! She's coming ! Don't let her see what I gave you. And go home right away and lock it up !

> (*He tiptoes away as if he were afraid of being found close to her and sits on the sofa at right, adopting a suspiciously careless attitude. Hazel looks self-conscious and stiff. Lavinia appears in the doorway and gives a start as she sees Hazel and Orin are alone. She quickly senses something in the atmosphere and glances sharply from one to the other as she comes into the room.*)

LAVINIA (*to Hazel, forcing a casual air*). I'm sorry I've been so long.

HAZEL. I didn't mind waiting.

LAVINIA (*sitting down on the chair at centre*). Where's Peter ?

HAZEL. He had to go to a Council meeting. He's coming back.

LAVINIA (*uneasiness creeping into her tone*). Has he been gone long ?

HAZEL. Not very long.

LAVINIA (*turning to Orin—sharply*). I thought you were in the study.

ORIN (*sensing her uneasiness—mockingly*). I finished what I was working on.

LAVINIA. You finished—— ? (*She glances sharply at Hazel—forcing a joking tone.*) My, but you two look mysterious ! What have you been up to ?

HAZEL (*trying to force a laugh*). Why, Vinnie ? What makes you think—— ?

LAVINIA. You're hiding something.

(*Hazel gives a start and instinctively moves the hand with the envelope farther behind her back. Lavinia notices this. So does Orin who uneasily comes to Hazel's rescue.*)

ORIN. We're not hiding anything. Hazel has

invited me over to their house to stay for a while—
and I'm going.

HAZEL (*backing him up resolutely*).　Yes.　Orin is
coming to-morrow.

LAVINIA (*alarmed and resentful—coldly*).　It's kind
of you.　I know you mean it for the best.　But he
can't go.

HAZEL (*sharply*).　Why not?

LAVINIA.　I don't care to discuss it, Hazel.
You ought to know——

HAZEL (*angrily*).　I don't know!　Orin is of
age and can go where he pleases!

ORIN.　Let her talk as she likes, Hazel.　I'll
have the upper hand for a change, from now on!
(*Lavinia looks at him, frightened by the triumphant
satisfaction in his voice.*)

HAZEL (*anxious to score her point and keep Orin's
mind on it*).　I should think you'd be glad.　It will
be the best thing in the world for him.

LAVINIA (*turns on her—angrily*).　I'll ask you to
please mind your own business, Hazel!

HAZEL (*springs to her feet, in her anger forgetting
to hide the envelope which she now holds openly in
her hand*).　It is my business!　I love Orin better
than you do!　I don't think you love him at all,
the way you've been acting!

THE HAUNTED

ORIN (*sees the envelope in plain sight and calls to her warningly*). Hazel ! (*She catches his eye and hastily puts her hand behind her. Lavinia sees the movement but doesn't for a moment realize the meaning of it. Orin goes on warningly.*) You said you had to go home early. I don't want to remind you but——

HAZEL (*hastily*). Yes, I really must. (*Starting to go, trying to keep the envelope hidden, aware that Lavinia is watching her suspiciously—defiantly to Orin.*) We'll expect you to-morrow, and have your room ready. (*Then to Lavinia—coldly.*) After the way you've insulted me, Vinnie, I hope you realize there's no more question of any friendship between us. (*She tries awkwardly to sidle towards the door.*)

LAVINIA (*suddenly gets between her and the door—with angry accusation*). What are you hiding behind your back ? (*Hazel flushes guiltily, but refusing to lie, says nothing. Lavinia turns on Orin.*) Have you given her what you've written ? (*As he hesitates—violently.*) Answer me !

ORIN. That's my business ! What if I have ?

LAVINIA. You—you traitor ! You coward ! (*Fiercely to Hazel.*) Give it to me ! Do you hear ?

HAZEL. Vinnie ! How dare you talk in that way to me ! (*She tries to go but Lavinia keeps directly between her and the door.*)

LAVINIA. You shan't leave here until——! (*Then breaking down and pleading.*) Orin! Think what you're doing! Tell her to give it to me!

ORIN. No!

LAVINIA (*goes and puts her arms around him— beseechingly as he avoids her eyes*). Think sanely for a moment! You can't do this! You're a Mannon!

ORIN (*harshly*). It's because I'm one!

LAVINIA. For Mother's sake, you can't! You loved her!

ORIN. A lot she cared! Don't call on her!

LAVINIA (*desperately*). For my sake, then! You know I love you! Make Hazel give that up and I'll do anything—anything you want me to!

ORIN (*stares into her eyes, bending his head until his face is close to hers—with morbid intensity*). You mean that?

LAVINIA (*shrinking back from him—falteringly*). Yes.

ORIN (*laughs with a crazy triumph—checks this abruptly—and goes to Hazel who has been standing, bewildered, not understanding what is behind their talk but sensing something sinister, and terribly frightened. Orin speaks curtly, his eyes fixed on Lavinia*). Let me have it, Hazel.

HAZEL (*hands him the envelope—in a trembling voice*). I'll go home. I suppose—we can't expect you to-morrow—now.

ORIN. No. Forget me. The Orin you loved was killed in the war. (*With a twisted smile.*) Remember only that dead hero and not his rotting ghost ! Good-bye ! (*Then harshly.*) Please go ! (*Hazel begins to sob and hurries blindly from the room. Orin comes back to Lavinia who remains kneeling by the chair. He puts the envelope in her hand—harshly.*) Here ! You realize the promise you made means giving up Peter ? And never seeing him again ?

LAVINIA (*tensely*). Yes.

ORIN. And I suppose you think that's all it means, that I'll be content with a promise I've forced out of you, which you'll always be plotting to break ? Oh, no ! I'm not such a fool ! I've got to be sure—— (*She doesn't reply or look at him. He stares at her and slowly a distorted look of desire comes over his face.*) You said you would do anything for me. That's a large promise, Vinnie—anything !

LAVINIA (*shrinking from him*). What do you mean ? What terrible thing have you been thinking lately—behind all your crazy talk ? No, I don't want to know ! Orin ! Why do you look at me like that ?

ORIN. You don't seem to feel all you mean to

me now—all you have made yourself mean—since we murdered Mother !

LAVINIA.   Orin !

ORIN.   I love you now with all the guilt in me— the guilt we share !   Perhaps I love you too much, Vinnie !

LAVINIA.   You don't know what you're saying !

ORIN.   There are times now when you don't seem to be my sister, nor Mother, but some stranger with the same beautiful hair——   (*He touches her hair caressingly.   She pulls violently away. He laughs wildly.*)   Perhaps you're Marie Brantôme, eh ?   And you say there are no ghosts in this house ?

LAVINIA (*staring at him with fascinated horror*). For God's sake—— !   No !   You're insane ! You can't mean—— !

ORIN.   How else can I be sure you won't leave me ?   You would never dare leave me—then ! You would feel as guilty then as I do !   You would be as damned as I am !   (*Then with sudden anger as he sees the growing horrified repulsion on her face.*)   Damn you, don't you see I must find some certainty some way or go mad ?   You don't want me to go mad, do you ?   I would talk too much !   I would confess !   (*Then as if the word stirred something within him his tone instantly changes to one of passionate pleading.*)   Vinnie !   For the love of God, let's go now and confess and pay the penalty for Mother's murder, and find peace together !

LAVINIA (*tempted and tortured, in a longing whisper*). Peace ! (*Then summoning her will, springs to her feet wildly.*) No ! You coward ! There is nothing to confess ! There was only justice !

ORIN (*turns and addresses the portraits on the wall with a crazy mockery*). You hear her ? You'll find Lavinia Mannon harder to break than me ! You'll have to haunt and hound her for a lifetime !

LAVINIA (*her control snapping—turning on him now in a burst of frantic hatred and rage*). I hate you ! I wish you were dead ! You're too vile to live ! You'd kill yourself if you weren't a coward !

ORIN (*starts back as if he'd been struck, the tortured, mad look on his face changing to a stricken, terrified expression*). Vinnie !

LAVINIA. I mean it ! I mean it ! (*She breaks down and sobs hysterically.*)

ORIN (*in a pitiful, pleading whisper*). Vinnie ! (*He stares at her with the lost, stricken expression for a moment more—then the obsessed wild look returns to his eyes—with harsh mockery.*) Another act of justice, eh ? You want to drive me to suicide as I drove Mother ! An eye for an eye, is that it ? But—— (*He stops abruptly and stares before him, as if this idea were suddenly taking hold of his tor-*

tured imagination, and speaks as if hypnotized.) Yes !
That would be justice—now you are Mother !
She is speaking now through you ! (*More and
more hypnotized by this train of thought.*) Yes ! It's
the way to peace—to find her again—my lost
island—Death is an Island of Peace, too—Mother
will be waiting for me there—— (*With excited
eagerness now, speaking to the dead.*) Mother ! Do
you know what I'll do then ? I'll get on my
knees and ask your forgiveness—and say—— (*His
mouth grows convulsed, as if he were retching up poison.*)
I'll say, I'm glad you found love, Mother ! I'll
wish you happiness—you and Adam ! (*He laughs
exultantly.*) You've heard me ! You're here in
the house now ! You're calling me ! You're
waiting to take me home ! (*He turns and strides
towards the door.*)

LAVINIA (*who has raised her head and has been
staring at him with dread during the latter part of
his talk—torn by remorse, runs after him and throws
her arms around him*). No, Orin ! No !

ORIN (*pushes her away—with a rough brotherly
irritation*). Get out of my way, can't you ? Mother's
waiting ! (*He gets to the door. Then he turns back
and says sharply:*) Ssshh ! Here's Peter ! Shut
up, now ! (*He steps back in the room as Peter
appears in the doorway.*)

PETER. Excuse my coming straight in. The
door was open. Where's Hazel ?

ORIN (*with unnatural casualness*). Gone home. (*Then with a quick, meaning, mocking glance at Lavinia.*) I'm just going in the study to clean my pistol. Darn thing's got so rusty. Glad you came now, Peter. You can keep Vinnie company. (*He turns and goes out the door. Peter stares after him, puzzled.*)

LAVINIA (*with a stifled cry*). Orin ! (*There is no answer but the sound of the study door being shut. She starts to run after him, stops herself, then throws herself into Peter's arms, as if for protection against herself, and begins to talk volubly to drown her thoughts.*) Hold me close, Peter ! Nothing matters but love, does it ? That must come first ! No price is too great, is it ? Oh, for peace ! One must have peace—one is too weak to forget—no one has the right to keep anyone from peace ! (*She makes a motion to cover her ears with her hands.*)

PETER (*alarmed by her hectic excitement*). He's a darned fool to monkey with a pistol—in his state. Shall I get it away from him ?

LAVINIA (*holding him tighter—volubly*). Oh, won't it be wonderful, Peter—once we're married and have a home with a garden and trees ! We'll be so happy ! I love everything that grows simply— up towards the sun—everything that's straight and strong ! I hate what's warped and twists and eats into itself and dies for a lifetime in shadow. (*Then her voice rising as if it were about to break hysterically—again with the instinctive movement to cover her ears.*) I can't bear waiting—waiting and waiting and waiting—— ! (*There is a muffled shot from the study across the hall.*)

PETER (*breaking from her and running for the door*). Good God ! What's that ? (*He rushes into the hall.*)

LAVINIA (*sags weakly and supports herself against the table—in a faint, trembling voice*). Orin ! Forgive me ! (*She controls herself with a terrible effort of will. Her mouth congeals into a frozen line. Mechanically she hides the sealed envelope in a drawer of the table and locks the drawer.*) I've got to go in—— (*She turns to go and her eyes catch the eyes of the Mannons in the portraits fixed accusingly on her—defiantly.*) Why do you look at me like that ? Wasn't it the only way to keep your secret, too ? But I've finished with you for ever now, do you hear ? I'm Mother's daughter—not one of you ! I'll live in spite of you !

> (*She squares her shoulders, with a return of the abrupt military movement copied from her father which she had of old —as if by the very act of disowning the Mannons she had returned to the fold— and marches stiffly from the room.*)

(*Curtain.*)

ACT FOUR

SCENE. *Same as Act One, Scene One—exterior of the house. It is in the late afternoon of a day three days later. The Mannon house has much the same appearance as it had in the first act of "Homecoming." Soft golden sunlight shimmers in a luminous mist on the Greek temple portico, intensifying the whiteness of the columns, the deep green of the shutters, the green of the shrubbery, the black and green of the pines. The columns cast black bars of shadow on the grey stone wall behind them. The shutters are all fastened back, the windows open. On the ground floor, the upper part of the windows, raised from the bottom, reflect the sun in a smouldering stare, as of brooding, revengeful eyes.*

Seth appears walking slowly up the drive from right front. He has a pair of grass clippers and potters along pretending to trim the edge of the lawn along the drive. But in reality he is merely killing time, chewing tobacco, and singing mournfully to himself, in his aged, plaintive wraith of a once good baritone, the chanty "Shenandoah":

SETH.

" *Oh, Shenandoah, I long to hear you*
A-way, my rolling river.
Oh, Shenandoah, I can't get near you
Way—ay, I'm bound away
Across the wide Missouri.

MOURNING BECOMES ELECTRA

" *Oh, Shenandoah, I love your daughter
A-way, you rolling river.*"

SETH (*stops singing and stands peering off left
towards the flower garden—shakes his head and mutters
to himself*).   There she be pickin' my flowers agin.
Like her Maw used to—on'y wuss.   She's got
every room in the house full of 'em a'ready.   Durn
it, I hoped she'd stop that once the funeral was over.
There won't be a one left in my garden !   (*He
looks away and begins pottering about again, and
mutters grimly.*)   A durn queer thin' fur a sodger
to kill himself cleanin' his gun, folks is sayin'.
They'll fight purty shy of her now.   A Mannon
has come to mean sudden death to 'em.   (*Then
with a grim pride.*)   But Vinnie's able fur 'em.
They'll never git her to show nothin'.   Clean
Mannon strain !

> (*Lavinia enters from the left.   The three days
> that have intervened have effected a
> remarkable change in her.   Her body,
> dressed in deep mourning, again appears
> flat-chested and thin.   The Mannon
> mask-semblance of her face appears in-
> tensified now.   It is deeply lined, haggard
> with sleeplessness and strain, congealed
> into a stony, emotionless expression.   Her
> lips are bloodless, drawn taut in a grim
> line.   She is carrying a large bunch of
> flowers.   She holds them out to Seth and
> speaks in a strange, empty voice.*)

LAVINIA. Take these, Seth, and give them to Hannah. Tell her to arrange them indoors. I want the house to be full of flowers. Peter is coming, and I want everything to be pretty and cheerful.

> (*She goes and sits at the top of the steps, bolt upright, her arms held stiffly to her sides, her legs and feet pressed together, and stares back into the sun-glare with un-blinking, frozen, defiant eyes.*)

SETH (*stands holding the flowers and regarding her anxiously*). I seed you settin' out here on the steps when I got up at five this mornin'—and every mornin' since Orin—— Ain't you been gittin' no sleep ? (*She stares before her as if she had not heard him. He goes on coaxingly.*) How'd you like if I hauled one of them sofas out fur you to lie on, Vinnie ? Mebbe you could take a couple o' winks an' it'd do you good.

LAVINIA. No, thank you, Seth. I'm waiting for Peter. (*Then after a pause, curiously.*) Why didn't you tell me to go in the house and lie down ? (*Seth pretends not to hear the question, avoiding her eyes.*) You understand, don't you ? You've been with us Mannons so long ! You know there's no rest in this house which Grandfather built as a temple of Hate and Death !

SETH (*blurts out*). Don't you try to live here, Vinnie ! You marry Peter and git clear !

LAVINIA. I'm going to marry him ! And I'm going away with him and will forget this house, and all that ever happened in it !

SETH. That's talkin', Vinnie !

LAVINIA. I'll close it up and leave it in the sun and rain to die. The portraits of the Mannons will rot on the walls and the ghosts will fade back into death. And the Mannons will be forgotten. I'm the last and I won't be one long. I'll be Mrs. Peter Niles. Then they're finished ! Thank God !

> (*She leans back in the sunlight and closes her eyes. Seth stares at her again, shakes his head and spits. Then he hears something and peers down the drive, off left.*)

SETH. Vinnie, here's Hazel comin'.

LAVINIA (*jerks up stiffly with a look of alarm*). Hazel ? What does she want ? (*She springs up as if she were going to run in the house, then stands her ground on the top of the steps—her voice hardening.*) Seth, you go on with your work, please !

SETH. Ayeh. (*He moves slowly off behind the lilacs as Hazel enters from left front—calling back.*) Evenin', Hazel.

HAZEL. Good evening, Seth.

> (*She stops short and stares at Lavinia. Lavinia's eyes are hard and defiant as*

she stares back. Hazel is dressed in mourning. Her face is sad and pale, her eyes show evidence of much weeping, but there is an air of stubborn resolution about her as she makes up her mind and walks to the foot of the steps.)

LAVINIA. What do you want? I've got a lot to attend to.

HAZEL (*quietly*). It won't take me long to say what I've come to say, Vinnie. (*Suddenly she bursts out.*) It's a lie about Orin killing himself by accident! I know it is! He meant to!

LAVINIA. You better be careful what you say. I can prove what happened. Peter was here——

HAZEL. I don't care what anyone says!

LAVINIA. I should think you'd be the last one to accuse Orin——

HAZEL. I'm not accusing him! Don't you dare say that! I'm accusing you! You drove him to it! Oh, I know I can't prove it—any more than I can prove a lot of things Orin hinted at! But I know terrible things must have happened—and that you're to blame for them, somehow!

LAVINIA (*concealing a start of fear—changing to a forced reproachful tone*). What would Orin think of you coming here the day of his funeral to accuse me of the sorrow that's afflicted our family?

HAZEL (*feeling guilty and at the same time defiant and sure she is right*). All right, Vinnie. I won't say anything more. But I know there's something —and so do you—something that was driving Orin crazy—— (*She breaks down and sobs.*) Poor Orin !

LAVINIA (*stares straight before her. Her lips twitch. In a stifled voice between her clenched teeth*). Don't—do that !

HAZEL (*controlling herself—after a pause*). I'm sorry. I didn't come to talk about Orin.

LAVINIA (*uneasily*). What did you come for ?

HAZEL. About Peter.

LAVINIA (*as if this were something she had been dreading—harshly*). You leave Peter and me alone !

HAZEL. I won't ! You're not going to marry Peter and ruin his life ! (*Pleading now.*) You can't ! Don't you see he could never be happy with you, that you'll only drag him into this terrible thing—whatever it is—and make him share it ?

LAVINIA. There is no terrible thing !

HAZEL. I know Peter can't believe evil of any-one, but living alone with you, married, you couldn't hide it, he'd get to feel what I feel. You could never be happy because it would come between you ! (*Pleading again.*) Oh, Vinnie, you've got to be fair to Peter ! You've got to consider his happiness—if you really love him !

LAVINIA (*hoarsely*). I do love him !

HAZEL. It has started already—his being made unhappy through you !

LAVINIA. You're lying !

HAZEL. He quarrelled with Mother last night when she tried to talk to him—the first time he ever did such a thing ! It isn't like Peter. You've changed him. He left home and went to the hotel to stay. He said he'd never speak to Mother or me again. He's always been such a wonderful son before—and brother. We three have been so happy. It's broken Mother's heart. All she does is sit and cry. (*Desperately.*) Oh, Vinnie, you can't do it ! You will be punished if you do ! Peter would get to hate you in the end !

LAVINIA. No !

HAZEL. Do you want to take the risk of driving Peter to do what Orin did ? He might—if he ever discovered the truth !

LAVINIA (*violently*). What truth, you little fool ! Discover what ?

HAZEL (*accusingly*). I don't know—but you know ! Look in your heart and ask your conscience before God if you ought to marry Peter !

LAVINIA (*desperately—at the end of her tether*).

Yes ! Before God ! Before anything ! (*Then glaring at her—with a burst of rage.*) You leave me alone—go away—or I'll get Orin's pistol and kill you ! (*Her rage passes, leaving her weak and shaken. She goes to her chair and sinks on it.*)

HAZEL (*recoiling*). Oh ! You are wicked ! I believe you would—— ! Vinnie ! What's made you like this ?

LAVINIA. Go away !

HAZEL. Vinnie ! (*Lavinia closes her eyes. Hazel stands staring at her. After a pause—in a trembling voice.*) All right. I'll go. All I can do is trust you. I know in your heart you can't be dead to all honour and justice—you, a Mannon ! (*Lavinia gives a little bitter laugh without opening her eyes.*) At least you owe it to Peter to let him read what Orin had in that envelope. Orin asked me to make him read it before he married you. I've told Peter about that, Vinnie.

LAVINIA (*without opening her eyes—strangely, as if to herself*). The dead ! Why can't the dead die !

HAZEL (*stares at her, frightened, not knowing what to do—looks around her uncertainly and sees someone coming from off left front—quickly*). Here he comes now. I'll go by the back. I don't want him to meet me. (*She starts to go but stops by the clump of lilacs—pityingly.*) I know you're suffering, Vinnie —and I know your conscience will make you do what's right—and God will forgive you. (*She goes quickly behind the lilacs and around the house to the rear.*)

LAVINIA (*looks after her and calls defiantly*). I'm not asking God or anybody for forgiveness. I forgive myself ! (*She leans back and closes her eyes again—bitterly.*) I hope there is a hell for the good somewhere !

> (*Peter enters from the left front. He looks haggard and tormented. He walks slowly, his eyes on the ground—then sees Lavinia and immediately makes an effort to pull himself together and appear cheerful.*)

PETER. Hello, Vinnie. (*He sits on the edge of the portico beside her. She still keeps her eyes closed, as if afraid to open them. He looks at her anxiously.*) You look terribly worn out. Haven't you slept ? (*He pats her hand with awkward tenderness. Her mouth twitches and draws down at the corners as she stifles a sob. He goes on comfortingly.*) You've had an awfully hard time of it, but never mind, we'll be married soon.

LAVINIA (*without opening her eyes—longingly*). You'll love me and keep me from remembering ?

PETER. You bet I will ! And the first thing is to get you away from this darned house ! I may be a fool but I'm beginning to feel superstitious about it myself.

LAVINIA (*without opening her eyes—strangely*).

Yes. Love can't live in it. We'll go away and leave it alone to die—and we'll forget the dead.

PETER (*a bitter, resentful note coming into his voice*). We can't move too far away to suit me ! I hate this damned town now and everyone in it !

LAVINIA (*startled, opens her eyes and looks at him*). I never heard you talk in that way before, Peter—bitter !

PETER (*avoiding her eyes*). Some things would make anyone bitter !

LAVINIA. You've quarrelled with your mother and Hazel—on account of me—is that it ?

PETER. How did you know ?

LAVINIA. Hazel was here just now.

PETER. She told you ? The darned fool ! What did she do that for ?

LAVINIA. She doesn't want me to marry you.

PETER (*angrily*). The little sneak ! What right has she——? (*Then a bit uneasily—forcing a smile.*) Well, you won't pay any attention to her, I hope.

LAVINIA (*more as if she were answering some voice in herself than him—stiffening in her chair—defiantly*). No !

PETER. She and Mother suddenly got a lot of crazy notions in their heads. But they'll get over them.

LAVINIA (*staring at him searchingly—uneasily*). Supposing they don't ?

PETER. They will after we are married—or I've done with them !

LAVINIA (*a pause. Then she takes his face in her hands and turns it to hers*). Peter ! Let me look at you ! You're suffering ! Your eyes have a hurt look ! They've always been so trustful ! They look suspicious and afraid of life now ! Have I done this to you already, Peter ? Are you beginning to suspect me ? Are you wondering what it was Orin wrote ?

PETER (*protesting violently*). No ! Of course I'm not ! Don't I know Orin was out of his mind ? Why should I pay any attention—— ?

LAVINIA. You swear you'll never suspect me—of anything ?

PETER. What do you think I am ?

LAVINIA. And you'll never let anyone come between us ? Nothing can keep us from being happy, can it ? You won't let anything, will you ?

PETER. Of course I won't !

LAVINIA (*more and more desperately*). I want to get married right away, Peter ! I'm afraid ! Would you marry me now—this evening ? We can find a minister to do it. I can change my

clothes in a second and put on the colour you like !
Marry me to-day, Peter ! ·I'm afraid to wait !

PETER (*bewildered and a bit shocked*). But—you
don't mean that, do you ? We couldn't. It
wouldn't look right the day Orin—out of respect
for him. (*Then suspicious in spite of himself.*) I
can't see why you're so afraid of waiting. Nothing
can happen, can it ? Was there anything in what
Orin wrote that would stop us from——— ?

LAVINIA (*with a wild beaten laugh*). The dead
coming between ! They always would, Peter !
You trust me with your happiness ! But that
means trusting the Mannon dead—and they're
not to be trusted with love ! I know them too
well ! And I couldn't bear to watch your eyes
grow bitter and hidden from me and wounded in
their trust of life ! I love you too much !

PETER (*made more uneasy and suspicious by this*).
What are you talking about, Vinnie ? You make
me think there was something———

LAVINIA (*desperately*). No—nothing ! (*Then
suddenly throwing her arms around him.*) No !
Don't think of that—not yet ! I want a little
while of happiness—in spite of all the dead !
I've earned it ! I've done enough——— ! (*Growing
more desperate—pleading wildly.*) Listen, Peter !
Why must we wait for marriage ? I want a moment
of joy—of love—to make up for what's coming !
I want it now ! Can't you be strong, Peter ?

Can't you be simple and pure ? Can't you forget sin and see that all love is beautiful ? (*She kisses him with desperate passion.*) Kiss me ! Hold me close ! Want me ! Want me so much you'd murder anyone to have me ! I did that—for you ! Take me in this house of the dead and love me ! Our love will drive the dead away ! It will shame them back into death ! (*At the topmost pitch of desperate, frantic abandonment.*) Want me ! Take me, Adam ! (*She is brought back to herself with a start by this name escaping her—bewildered, laughing idiotically.*) Adam ? Why did I call you Adam ? I never even heard that name before—outside the Bible ! (*Then suddenly with a hopeless, dead finality.*) Always the dead between ! It's no good trying any more !

PETER (*convinced she is hysterical and yet shocked and repelled by her display of passion*). Vinnie ! You're talking crazy ! You don't know what you're saying ! You're not—like that !

LAVINIA (*in a dead voice*). I can't marry you, Peter. You mustn't ever see me again. (*He stares at her, stunned and stupid.*) Go home. Make it up with your mother and Hazel. Marry someone else. Love isn't permitted to me. The dead are too strong !

PETER (*his mind in a turmoil*). Vinnie ! You can't—— ! You've gone crazy—— ! What's changed you like this ? (*Then suspiciously.*) Is it—what Orin wrote ? What was it ? I've got a right to know, haven't I ? (*Then as she doesn't answer—more suspiciously.*) He acted so queerly about—what happened to you on the Islands. Was it something there—something to do with that native—— ?

LAVINIA (*her first instinctive reaction one of hurt insult*). Peter ! Don't you dare—— ! (*Then suddenly seizing on this as a way out—with calculated coarseness.*) All right ! Yes, if you must know ! I won't lie any more ! Orin suspected I'd lusted with him ! And I had !

PETER (*shrinking from her, aghast—brokenly*). Vinnie ! You've gone crazy ! I don't believe—— You—you couldn't !

LAVINIA (*stridently*). Why shouldn't I ? I wanted him ! I wanted to learn love from him—love that wasn't a sin ! And I did, I tell you ! He had me ! I was his fancy woman !

PETER (*wincing as if she had struck him in the face, stares at her with a stricken look of horrified repulsion—with bitter, broken anger*). Then—Mother and Hazel were right about you—you are bad at heart—no wonder Orin killed himself—God, I—I hope you'll be punished—I—— ! (*He hurries blindly off down the drive to the left.*)

LAVINIA (*watches him go—then with a little desperate cry starts after him*). Peter ! It's a lie ! I didn't—— ! (*She stops abruptly and stiffens into her old square-shouldered attitude. She looks down*

*the drive after him—then turns away, saying in a
lost, empty tone.)* Good-bye, Peter.

> (*Seth enters from the left rear, coming round
> the corner of the house. He stands for
> a moment watching her, grimly wonder-
> ing. Then to call her attention to his
> presence, he begins singing half under
> his breath his melancholy " Shenandoah "
> chanty, at the same time looking at the
> ground around him as if searching for
> something.*)

SETH. " *Oh, Shenandoah, I can't get near you
    Way—ay, I'm bound away———*"

LAVINIA (*without looking at him, picking up the
words of the chanty—with a grim writhen smile*).
I'm not bound away—not now, Seth. I'm bound
here—to the Mannon dead ! (*She gives a dry little
cackle of laughter and turns as if to enter the house.*)

SETH (*frightened by the look on her face, grabs her
by the arm*). Don't go in there, Vinnie !

LAVINIA (*grimly*). Don't be afraid. I'm not
going the way Mother and Orin went. That's
escaping punishment. And there's no one left to
punish me. I'm the last Mannon. I've got to
punish myself ! Living alone here with the dead
is a worse act of justice than death or prison !
I'll never go out or see anyone ! I'll have the
shutters nailed close so no sunlight can ever get
in. I'll live alone with the dead, and keep their

287

secrets, and let them hound me, until the curse is paid out and the last Mannon is let die ! (*With a strange cruel smile of gloating over the years of self-torture.*) I know they will see to it I live for a long time ! It takes the Mannons to punish themselves for being born !

SETH (*with grim understanding*). Ayeh. And I ain't heard a word you've been sayin', Vinnie. (*Pretending to search the ground again.*) Left my clippers around somewheres.

LAVINIA (*turns to him sharply*). You go now and close the shutters and nail them tight.

SETH. Ayeh.

LAVINIA. And tell Hannah to throw out all the flowers.

SETH. Ay

> (*He goes past her up the steps and into the house. She ascends to the portico—and then turns and stands for a while, stiff and square-shouldered, staring into the sunlight with frozen eyes. Seth leans out of the window at the right of the door and pulls the shutters close with a decisive bang. As if this were a word of command, Lavinia pivots sharply on her heel and marches woodenly into the house, closing the door behind her.*)

(*Curtain.*)

JONATHAN CAPE PAPERBACKS